BORN OUT OF THIS

Caitlin Press Inc.
8100 Alderwood Road,
Halfmoon Bay, BC V0N 1Y1
www.caitlin-press.com

Edited by Jane Silcott
Text and cover design by Vici Johnstone
Cover photograph copyright Vici Johnstone
All photos unless otherwise noted are copyright Christine Lowther. The photographers for the images on pages 15, 86, 160 and 183 are unknown. Source unknown for the referenced flyer on page 93. D.O.A. is the source of the flyer on page 132. All possible efforts were made to source the creators of uncredited material.
Printed in Canada

Caitlin Press Inc. acknowledges financial support from the Government of Canada through the Canada Book Fund and the Canada Council for the Arts, and from the Province of British Columbia through the British Columbia Arts Council and the Book Publisher's Tax Credit.

Canada Council   Conseil des Arts
for the Arts   du Canada

BRITISH COLUMBIA
ARTS COUNCIL

Library and Archives Canada Cataloguing in Publication

Lowther, Christine, author
    Born out of this : a memoir / Christine Lowther.

ISBN 978-1-927575-55-0 (pbk.)

    1. Lowther, Christine. 2. Lowther, Pat, 1935-1975.
3. Poets, Canadian (English)—20th century—Biography. I. Title.

PS8573.O898Z53 2014   C811'.54   C2014-904119-5

BORN
OUT
OF
THIS

CHRISTINE LOWTHER

CAITLIN PRESS

Books by Christine Lowther

Half-Blood Poems: Inspired by the Stories of J.K. Rowling (Hamden, CT: Zossima Press, 2011)

My Nature (Lantzville, BC: Leaf Press, 2010)

New Power (Fredericton, NB: Broken Jaw Press, 1999)

Books edited by Christine Lowther

Writing the West Coast: In Love With Place, co-edited with Anita Sinner, (Vancouver, BC: Ronsdale Press, 2008)

Living Artfully: Reflections from the Far West Coast, co-edited with Anita Sinner, (Toronto, ON: Key Publishing House Inc., 2012)

Some of the essays in this book have been previously published.

For Beth and Kathy.

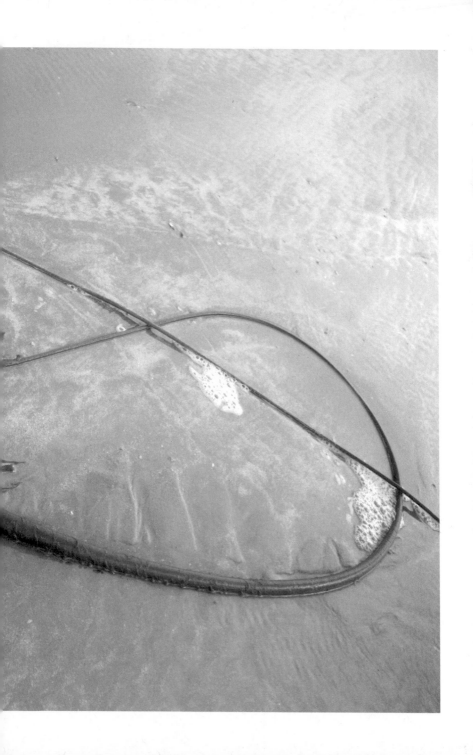

CONTENTS

PART 1
FLOATING SEASON

THE SPAWNING GROUNDS

As we near the creek mouth, I pull back on the throttle and keep both eyes on the bay's muddy bottom until it's time to raise the propeller. A small seal cruises out of our way, observing us with dark eyes. My two friends and I use paddles to pull us forward until the boat grounds on the mud, then wait for the quickly rising tide to nudge us to shore.

This is a time to look and listen. The bay echoes with gulls' cries, and we are absorbed by their choreography of sound and motion until we spy a slow salmon's fin or tail breaking the water's surface. We study the shallows around us for more of the dark gliding fishes. An eagle emerges from the forest and soars overhead, calling.

As our boat settles in soft mud, the unperturbed gulls walk or fly to the far side of the grassy estuary. They continue to feast on salmon parts; scattered bones lie over the grass. Here a severed vertebra, there a jaw with formidable-looking teeth and back here, a disembodied tail.

For one moment the birds quiet down and the still air is pierced by the wild cry of a red-tailed hawk. We humans all look at each other wide-eyed and jump out in our gumboots to carry the anchor to shore. "Let's make sure it doesn't end up under water," someone says.

Dozens of yellow bodies choke the low stream. These are big chum salmon. Many are missing sections. Often I come across empty skins, as if they were shed like a snake's. What predator dislikes salmon skins? How does it remove them so neatly? Some are draped over low branches, like shirts laid carefully to dry.

Barely submerged, the living move slowly among the dead, except for sudden splashes, bursts of energy, pinnacles of desperation. There hasn't been enough rain to swell the stream, so the salmon cannot travel any distance up the creek. Many are half out of the water, struggling to keep their noses under. As they make their street-gang ambushes, trying to take over thin pools crowded with the dead, I glance up at the cloudless sky between the trees and yearn for rain. I want the rainforest to live up to its name.

Near the forest wall the stench is too much for me. I turn back in time to see the hawk fly to a convenient branch, then take careful sidesteps along it. Its cries are darts through the air, shots of adrenalin. I almost step on a bear scat full of what looks like salmon roe. Next to it is a carcass with its middle cleanly removed. This landscape of gore nourishes and fertilizes the trees and berry bushes.

I come to a stop and look around for my friends. Julie is near the shoreline gazing into the trees, probably at the hawk. Maryjka is nearer to me, watching the drama at her feet. We are three humans standing between forest and ocean like acupuncture needles, feeling the world pulsing with its endless cycles. The water-dwellers we're here to see have been returning to spawn in this place for thousands of years.

I walk along the stream toward the boat and come across the bright yellow, two-and-a-half-foot-long body of a dog salmon, its empty eye socket a pool of blood. When I shift to step over it, it makes a slow slippery movement. Still alive.

The hawk flies over and perches in a tall, skinny, leafless alder, watching the salmon and me, waiting for us humans to leave. I lift the anchor, dripping and heavy, from the water and we hoist ourselves on board. I've collected a few dead in a bucket to feed the soil of my garden. Slowly we paddle for deeper water as the seal returns, turning its head to watch us go. Behind us is Lone Cone; ahead, Mount Colnett.

The next day pours rain.

GIFTS FROM LANDS SO FAR APART

Isabella Road on Mayne Island is named for a North Vancouver girl-turned-vaudeville-star, a great-aunt I never met. Wilkes Road, mistakenly including an "e" my family never used, is named after one of Isabella's younger brothers, my great-uncle Bill Wilks, who purchased land here from the government. (He paid ten dollars.) However you spell it, to me Wilks is a beautiful, liquid name. Other names on this island are equally pleasing: Fernhill, Sunset, Wood Dale, Orchard, Arbutus.

In the early 1970s, every summer for a week or so we came to Mayne: my parents, my sister Beth and me. We stayed in a two-room cabin called Sleepy Hollow on Uncle Bill's land at Bennett Bay. Here we peered from the arbutus and Douglas fir woods onto a field stretching down to the beach. Small, round, forest-cloaked islands squatted on the water like shaggy mushroom caps. In a letter to a friend, my mother mused:

The [Gulf] Islands are incredibly beautiful, though I suppose they'll inevitably be spoiled by the sub-dividing that's going on now. Still, some things can't be changed, like the view from the cabin, which looks out on a bay and chains of beautifully shaped small islands.

My mother had read her poems at peace rallies while we each took our turn in her womb. And she taught us to protest the needless destruction of trees. Lion strength radiated from *Arbutus menziesii* the first time I hugged a tree. When Mum and a friend on Prince Edward Island exchanged gifts via Canada Post, we received a sample of red soil from that distant island province, and Mum sent pieces of arbutus bark. The gifts, from lands so far apart, shared the same colour.

In those days children were not so fearfully guarded, and I liked going solo, sprinting down the field to the beach. I sought the shore's sun-heated stonescape, what Mum described as "skulls of rock"[1] in her poetry. To cool off I entered the woods, where the ground was littered with papery peels of warm red arbutus bark, which curled away from the trunks to reveal cool, smooth green—I want to say *skin*. "Arbutus lifting their bodies like poems"[2] were an integral part of the island's magic. Their large leaves snapped "like thin glass underfoot."[3] Uncle Bill's ten-dollar plot of land included an eleven-acre peninsula full of them, trunks careening gracefully in every known and unimagined direction, inventing their own fantastic inner compass: a not-so-civilized arrhythmic dance that mocked the stiff, undeviating uprightness of neighbouring firs.

This was the first place to imprint itself onto my heart: while my

---

1   Pat Lowther, untitled. Previously unpublished.
2   Pat Lowther, "Stereoscopy: An Island," in *The Collected Works of Pat Lowther*, ed. Christine Wiesenthal (Edmonton: NeWest Press, 2010).
3   Ibid.

city was grey with a nighttime refrain of ambulance sirens, Mayne was quiet and softly coloured, and warmed me from the inside. The autumn when my father brought my sister Beth and me, it had changed. The island ached with our mother's unexplained absence, the grey had followed us and rain poured down from an ill-omened, clay sky. We weren't staying in Sleepy Hollow, either. We were put to bed in an unfamiliar single-room rental cabin across the road instead.

The bed Beth and I shared was held to the ceiling by chains. As our two cats tried to get used to their new confined environment, our father held two saucepans up to us. We obediently vomited into them. My theory about why we were sick is that we were all living on junk food, his lifelong addiction and means of controlling us. We girls sat on the couch as he paced and paced, finally standing still to tell us our mother was dead. And those are my vague memories of our last days together. My mind, it seems, blocked out nearly all the rest.

Next thing I remember, we were left in the temporary care of a kind nudist woman who kept goats. We began attending a tiny school where all the grades were taught in one classroom. One of my classmates hurled a jagged rock at my face, hitting the left temple, just missing my eye. As the blood ran down, I felt shocked that a piece of my beloved island could cause such injury. But I forgave it, because it did not blind me. In time, I came to see the incident as a miracle.

It must have been October or November 1975 when my sister and I were pulled from our father's arms on the dock at Miner's Bay, the scab beside my eye perhaps still fresh. A police vessel transported us to a Victoria foster home where I sought solace in books and the wildest backyard I had ever seen in a city. Long grass clothed the earth, lying nearly flat on ground that banked steeply away from the house. Arbutus twisted downward out of it, straining as if to follow the tilt of the land. Oak trees grew there too. We rolled down the slope, hugged by the grass, feeling as if a piece of Uncle Bill's country had followed us. And while this was something of an adventure, no matter how kindly our hosts treated us we felt uncomfortable. We never saw our cats again.

My mother's mother retrieved us, on foot. She was sixty-eight and hauling our suitcases around despite a heart condition. At first the authorities refused to approve her plan. Then one bureaucrat finally offered to look the other way while Gram herded us to the ferry as quickly as she could. She told me all of this years later, of course, since I don't remember. My blocked mind takes me from Victoria to state care on the mainland without explanation.

Foster homes in North Vancouver were, thankfully, much closer to Gram. At a Lynn Valley home, as soon as we were left alone with the new family, we found ourselves on our knees in a prayer circle, and things got progressively more prickly from then on. When our older half-sister from Mum's first marriage, Kathy, heard we were living with religious fanatics she came screeching over in her Pontiac all the way from Duncan. Beth and I were playing in the front yard when she came to a halt at the curb. We dropped everything and hurled ourselves joyfully toward the car. I'm told I didn't bother stopping to open the car door. I leapt through the open window. When our foster mother ran outside demanding to know what was happening, Kathy called out that she was taking us for the day. When the woman protested, Kathy yelled "Fuck you! I'm their sister," and flipped her the finger as we peeled away.

Eventually we moved in with Gram, and then Beth and I were separated. We couldn't get along, even when my aunt included us in her summer holidays to a Cultus Lake trailer park. Taking us to Cultus was truly generous and I'm sure we were a pain in everybody's ass. They might not have known, but I was enchanted by the woods there. Later I spent a metamorphic year in a group home: boys, drugs, writing, a suicide attempt and rebirth through activism. I had chosen that place over Gram's home, at thirteen. When escape from it became necessary, she did not hesitate to welcome me back. Most of my teenage years were locked in a generation gap with Gram. I should have been more grateful, but I don't know that I could have been. Maybe I was too damaged to give her the gratitude she deserved.

From Gram's I daytripped by bus or bicycle to Lynn Canyon, Grouse Mountain and Mosquito Creek with its waterfall and enormous juicy salmonberries, where everywhere I looked I saw Emily Carr paintings. Then there was Lynn Headwaters Park, encompassing Rice Lake, where my grandfather was reservoir caretaker for six years during the early 1930s when the lake supplied Vancouver's drinking water. My mother was his first child; she spent the earliest years of her life in the bush, and remembered them well:

> When I was a child
> my father worked with water,
> adjusting flow and level,
> going out from his bed
> into 3 in the morning storms
> to keep the screens clear
> And once he took me to Rice Lake
> where no one is allowed—
> the water was flat as pavement
> papered with fallen leaves
> and flat wooden walkways
> and there I walked on water ...[4]

---

4   Pat Lowther, "In the Continent Behind My Eyes," in *Milk Stone* (Ottawa: Borealis Press, 1974). Recently published in *The Collected Works of Pat Lowther*, ed. Christine Wiesenthal.

My mother may have loved it there, but *her* mum couldn't have been less suited to life on the untamed North Shore. A younger sister of the vaudevillian Isabella, Gram had spent her youth dancing as a Roxyette chorus line girl under bright lights in lively American cities, and she wasn't crazy about the new isolation. So the family moved to lower Lonsdale Avenue, where my grandfather found work as a sheet metal worker in the harbourfront shipyard. He did this despite knowing that his father had died a gruesome death in 1923 at work in the bowels of the SS *Niagara*. Accidental work-related deaths were a legacy my grandparents had in common. Gram's dad became a union activist after his own father had perished in a coal mine explosion in Nanaimo in 1888. The unfortunate man had come to Canada to escape northern England's colliery life.

I had no real awareness of our working class status while living with Gram and my uncles in the small kit house Grampa had built. Throughout my secondary school years, we never had a car and did not travel. I could hardly imagine the places so many of my high-school peers had been, and was impressed by the historical architecture we studied in Civilizations class. After high school I lived with roommates and went to college, which was paid for by the government until my nineteenth birthday, when an unexpected five-thousand-dollar "criminal injustice award" crystallized. By this time I sported a striped mohawk and was deeply into Vancouver's punk scene. Yet this was my chance to expand; I knew I wouldn't be buying college courses with that money. A cousin suggested I invest, but that might require staying. Escape and adventure were within my grasp. For the first time in my life, I left the country, the continent, my education and everybody I knew behind.

In Britain I nourished my romantic inclinations with art and cathedrals, Roman ruins and rural landscapes dotted with standing stones and holy wells. I travelled, joined the British Trust for Conservation

Volunteers and signed up for a National Certificate in Countryside-Related Studies at a college in Shropshire. This called for a variety of endeavours including driving a tractor, building fences in horizontal rain, studying habitat restoration and getting a rock chip wedged in my left cornea while practising traditional drystone walling. The land wounding me again—in the same eye. Maybe it was teaching me to look properly. One day, near Arundel Castle, West Sussex, I came face to face with an imported arbutus tree. I stood winded, blinking dumbly up at it.

In the UK people were getting arrested for trying to protect the odd 250-year-old chestnut tree, usually on a motorway roundabout or next to a rundown council estate. Back in BC, where I was ready to return after five years away, trees could be ancient. In the Walbran Valley on Vancouver Island, there are immense western red cedars, some believed to be as old as two thousand years, with moss thick as castle walls growing on them. Too wet and dense for arbutus—dark and impenetrable—where young softwood saplings cannibalize their fallen forebears, the temperate rainforest is rich and multi-storeyed. It is the result of ten thousand years of evolution. A carbon-sink sponge of a jungle, it is the self-regulating home to countless weird and wonderful species: plants, insects, fungi and megafauna. I had never heard of Canada's rainforest before 1991. I didn't know it then, but the Walbran also hosts species at risk like the long-eared myotis (a bat), the Vaux's swift, the Queen Charlotte goshawk, and threatened runs of coho salmon. Furthermore, the air is free of the pulp mill musk common to the Gulf Islands.

And British Columbians were clearcutting this valley for Fletcher Challenge, a New Zealand corporation.

The Walbran was the setting of my first blockade, first skinny-dip, first completely uncivilized experience outside the mosh pit of a punk rock show. Why did I love the freezing river, the white falls, the tadpoles, salamanders, dippers and kingfishers? Because they are mysteries independent of us. They are *other* and in danger. In the words of the late Catherine Lebredt (who was writing about an area north of the Walbran, Clayoquot Sound): "There are times when the fragility of this beautiful place really hits me in the face."[5] It is no wonder that European settlers were terrified and couldn't wait to transform the unkempt frontier into tree farms and quaint, controlled gardens that reminded them of home. As my mum wrote,

> Imagine that I contain
>   branch   tree
>   butterflies   snakes
> the entire forest[6]

I settled on the Clayoquot coast, some miles north of the Walbran but still Rainforest Central. After ten years in my new ecosystem, where I was writing poems that dealt with my past, a filmmaker called Anne Henderson proposed a documentary showcasing my mother's life, death and poems, and the lives of my sisters and me. Would I like to re-embark on my youth's interminable odyssey, this time by choice? I saw it as further opportunity to heal and agreed.

In the film the present was as important as the past: Beth's home turf in Vancouver's east end, my home in downtown Tofino, the log cabin I'd lived in for a few years and the floathouse I have now—all were to become scenes or interview backdrops. But when Anne decided to shoot our father's hometown, Beth refused to come. He had, after all, been convicted of our mother's murder. Did consenting to travel there imply associating with the man? Could it indicate interest in or

5   Catherine Lebredt, "A Collection," in *Writing the West Coast: In Love With Place*, ed. Anita Sinner and Christine Lowther (Vancouver, BC: Ronsdale Press, 2008).
6   Pat Lowther, untitled. Previously unpublished.

even sympathy for him? In some way it felt like his birthplace was to blame for his actions, and merely visiting the locale could suggest an alliance. This was not the first time I was struck by the power of place. But that's not what she was thinking. Today, Beth explains, "I objected, in a film about his victim, to participating in a segment depicting us exploring his personal history which would be publicly viewed by her friends and family."

Selfishly, perhaps, I was fascinated with uncovering secrets of our past, keenly consumed with learning about my origins. I felt any morsel of information had the potential to help me. So I went. I had passed Britannia Beach a handful of times on my way to Squamish or Whistler. Britannia Mine Workings' famous landmark, the concentrator, dominates the town to this day. Built to take advantage of gravity, it covers an entire hillside, obliterating nature under monstrous steps, like Zeus's staircase except that instead of being made of gold, the concentrator, when I saw it in 2002, was a rusting wreck with broken windows. Venturing inside to meet the film crew, I goggled at an industrial chamber of horrors: tentacular cables reaching down from a ceiling invisible in the high darkness, the marred cliff wall stained copper-bronze, continual echoes of dripping water and moss growing doggedly in clumps. Our Québécois cameraman, Marc, frowned up at hundreds of worn, irregular wooden steps that careened steeply out of sight, a vertigo sufferer's nightmare. "My God," he muttered. "Stairway to 'Eaven."

My father's father worked for the mine in his youth and was its poet "laird" in his old age. My father also fancied himself a poet and loved nature. He fled the colliery life and escaped to university before becoming a destroyer of lives. The place that spawned him vomited forth a river so toxic that, according to locals, there was a plan to seal the opening—which spewed sulphide-poisoned acidic mineral water from the ravaged mountain—with a large cement cork. The mine was now one of the worst polluters in all of North America. A dubious heritage, indeed.

(Since our visit, a water treatment plant has been installed.)

The town itself proved an interesting and pleasant place, surviving off tourism, television and film. There were fewer than three hundred people living there and they all had a view of the ocean. My father's childhood house was otherwise unremarkable—inhabited by strangers, the neglected roof green with moss. Everyone we met was friendly. And behind the community, deep in the bush, three miles down what could only loosely be called a road, teetering railway bridges burned black amid other ruins. This was the old townsite of the workers. The one remaining building sheltered some towering mechanical dinosaur, idle since the mine's closure decades ago. Heaps of rubble were slowly being overtaken by alder trees, and I beheld the eerie fragments of a forgotten world, one I'd never known I came from.

A concrete doorway stood in the centre of the wide, shallow river, fabulous, surrealistic and pointless *punk shui*, waiting to crumble or be swept away. Yet full of potential: if I waded across the water and dared step through, it seemed I could end up almost anywhere: past, present or future, this cosmos or another.

Anne wanted to film a scene at nearby Furry Creek before heading back to Vancouver. I had no desire to see the place where my mother's body had been found three weeks after her murder, so I decamped, thinking of her poem about Furry Creek. The family had picnicked there when I was small, though I could not recall the "water reflecting cedars / all the way up / deep sonorous green...."[7]

She was thrown from a bridge. I imagine the soft autumn air consciously slowing her descent, cushioning, until she came to rest in "novocaine-cold"[8] water. There would have been no more blood, just

---

7   Pat Lowther's "Notes From Furry Creek" was originally published in *A Stone Diary* (Toronto: Oxford University Press, 1977). Later, it was published in *Time Capsule: New and Selected Poems* (Vancouver: Polestar, 1996). The book's cover shows close-ups of peeling arbutus and stone. Recently published in *The Collected Works of Pat Lowther*, ed. Christine Wiesenthal.

8   Ibid.

... the huckleberries
hanging
like fat red lanterns[9]

their bushes bowing in respect and grief. On October 13, 1975, a hiker stumbled upon her remains half-concealed under a log.

In 1999 author Keith Harrison produced a non-fiction novel, *Furry Creek*. In it, the soul who found her sits trembling in a police car wondering if "Furry" is meant to be "Fir-y": tall Douglas firs stood with the cedars and alders around the creek. Perhaps "Furry" described moss cloaking creek stones. My mother always noticed rock formations and stones:

When the stones swallowed me
I could not surface
but squatted
in foaming water
all one curve
motionless,
glowing like agate.[10]

She finished the poem by describing stone as "the perpetual / lavèd god."

Britannia Beach did not make the film's final cut, and I was fine with that. Beth had objected to its inclusion "on feminist grounds," and I had said no to being filmed looking at pictures of my father. Furry Creek has since been forever altered by golf courses and condominiums. Nevertheless, the last scene in the finished documentary, *Water Marks*, shows the creek flowing into Howe Sound.

---

9   Ibid.
10   Ibid.

The next stop was Mayne Island, where Beth and I were to be interviewed on the site of Sleepy Hollow (long gone), in the field at Bennett Bay and on Miner's Bay dock, where I had been forcibly pulled from my father's arms. More than twenty-five years had passed since Uncle Bill had helped detectives find the body with his homemade divining wire and a few hairs taken from Mum's brush (the hiker had simply arrived first). Uncle Bill was long dead. Gram had passed away in 1998 at the age of ninety. I had not seen my father since he stood weeping on the dock as we sped from him in the police boat. He died in prison ten years later.

It had been many years since either of us had set foot on Mayne. Now I knew it also as *Elelen*, its lovely, liquid Hul'qumi'num name. Bill's descendants had put his arbutus-covered peninsula up for sale; the provincial government made an offer, and turned it into parkland. Cameraman Marc fell in love with the island. I overheard him in a phone booth passionately describing its virtues to his girlfriend back in Québec. One of the words I recognized was "arbutus," repeated many times.

Perhaps the strangest shoot was at Miner's Bay. I had buried the memory of being torn from my father until it surfaced one afternoon in my twenties during some group peer counselling. Now here we were—two mature women in our thirties, long knowing what he was—calmly talking about it on a fine summer day for a film crew.

We both had mixed feelings about the film when it was released. It was shown on CBC Newsworld and the Knowledge Network. Shelagh Rogers interviewed us on national radio, and for months it seemed residents of Tofino were coming up to me on the street saying, "Saw you on TV last night!" Soon Beth and I agreed we never wanted to watch it again. I wasn't crazy about some of our interactions as markedly differing personalities, and then there were my regrettable hairstyle and clothing choices. More seriously, I think some family members were upset by some of the content—or by what wasn't said. After many years, I caught the first half hour of it again; some moments could be said to lean toward sensationalism. What's important is that my mother's story is told and that people never become complacent about violence against women and children.

As a child, and later a teen, I had promised myself I would live on Mayne someday. I liked thinking of my spinster aunt of fleeting vaudeville fame who had found immortality on a street sign. I still have kind and gracious relatives there, as well as the view of the bay and its small forested islands, as my mother had hoped. Yet, Mayne is like everywhere. As Marie Elliot writes in *Mayne Island*, "[a] dramatic confrontation between country and city is occurring ... as rural communities face the threat of urban assimilation."[11]

Sounds like home. Still, I miss the red, shedding trees in their atavistic poses, try to follow their example—keep to the littoral zone, reinvent my own inner compass. The place where I've ended up is wetter, chillier and, with its coniferous forests, a tad more abrasive. Though I barely knew my mother, I feel certain she would have loved it.

---

11   Marie Elliot, *Mayne Island and the Outer Gulf Islands* (Mayne Island, BC: Gulf Islands Press, 1984).

Destination Gratitude

An infant harbour seal cries for its mother on the rocks flanking my neighbour's oyster farm. I pause to listen, the cold water enflaming my skin. I am swimming at night for the first time. Scissoring my arms and legs, I make angels with the ocean's bioluminescence, comet-tails streaming between my fingers. Floating on my back, I know what Mum meant in her poem "Song" about feeling the galaxy on our cheeks and foreheads.

Later, as I fall into bed, barred owls call to each other in the forest. The seal has ceased its cries. My bed is level with the open window; as I face Lone Cone Mountain, my hip and shoulder mimic the curved contours of the land. A stanza from another of her poems comes to me:

> And nights when
> clouds foam on a beach
> of clear night sky,
> those high slopes creak
> in companionable sleep[12]

The last sound I hear before sleep, and the first one upon waking next morning, is of fish nipping at insects, repeatedly breaking the water's surface for a fraction of a second.

---

12   Pat Lowther, "Coast Range," in *A Stone Diary*. Recently published in *The Collected Works of Pat Lowther*, ed. Christine Wiesenthal.

‿

A friend once said to me, "You're the right sort of person to live the way you do, because you are obviously deeply affected by your surroundings." My immediate surroundings are deep, and wet. I live in a floathouse: a cabin that floats upon the sea. Under the summer sun, I immerse myself in water, alternating between hot tub and cold ocean. If I am kept from this ritual, spending too much time in town, extreme grumpiness ensues. The streets are choked with tourists, friendly, relaxed people whom I've been serving all day. It is in town where I am marooned; it is out here, seven kilometres up an inlet, where I relax.

Out. Here.

Here is the Tla-o-qui-aht traditional territory of Meares Island: *Wah-nah-jus–Hilth-hoo-is*. Visitors to the area know Meares for its Big Trees Trail, a boardwalk along huge ancient cedars. Meares is also special for never having been clearcut, apart from a patch on one of its mountains, the seven-hundred-thirty-metre Lone Cone. After Aboriginal and other local people turned loggers away in 1984, the Tla-o-qui-aht First Nation (TFN) declared Meares a Tribal Park. "Officially," it remains tied up in court with lengthy treaty processes and is the only grey area (literally) on the brightly colour-coded map of Clayoquot Sound. But by making tribal parks, the TFN defies treaty process and defends its land when provincial and other authorities will not. All of the Sound is a UNESCO-designated biosphere reserve, yet it remains unprotected from any industry, from logging to fish farming and mining.

One of the island's small coves encircles my floathome, snugly embracing it. The Tla-o-qui-ahts used to dig for clams here at low tide, but non-native oysters colonize the mud now, and sadly, the people whose land this is no longer come to this little bay and dig for food.

For many of us, it is a struggle to make Clayoquot Sound our home. Other than squatting, floating is arguably the only affordable way to live in the district of Tofino, a holidayer's mecca on Vancouver Island's west coast.

My commuting choices are an hour and a half in a scratched old kayak or twenty minutes in a barnacle-infested motorboat. In a storm, the motorboat's the only choice, and those twenty minutes can be the longest of one's life. Once I arrive, there is nowhere else to go, not even for a stroll. Four ropes, about ninety metres long, anchor the floathouse to the forested shore, where black bears sometimes meander, munching on shore grass, salal berries and huckleberries. Rarely, they'll take a dip, but they are not interested in humans. Three or four anchors keep me more or less in place.

How did I come to live here, in a house I named "Gratitude" to express my thankfulness to both the TFN and the place itself? It's simple. My then-partner and I needed a place to live.

Activism brought me here. My first involvement in direct action for Vancouver Island's forests was for the Walbran Valley in '91. It took hours on a rough logging road surrounded by clearcut moonscapes to reach what had been the traditional territory of the Pacheedaht people. Hiking past waterfalls on the Walbran River, I gaped at creamy Daliesque canyon walls reflected in jade-green water. Beyond a campsite dubbed Giggling Spruce, a landlocked lake supported its own exclusive species of trout. Some of the cedars were natural works of art. With their gargantuan candelabra crowns, they looked like multi-headed elephants, every trunk raised.

> When I said "Tree"
> my skin grew rough as bark.
> I almost remember how all the leaves

rushed shouting shimmering
out of my veins.[13]

As scientists searched for endangered marbled murrelets and activists gave tree-climbing workshops, I began to feel at home in the
rainforest. There were more roots here than anywhere. Minor addic-
tions fell away. Poems about roots and bugs seemed to write themselves. An unmistakable sensation of time slowing down permeated
my blood, and a week went by without a mirror. Being an inhabitant
for ten days of an ecosystem that took ten thousand years to evolve
stretched and calmed my mind. The "curly opaque Pacific / forest,
chilling you full awake / with wet branch-slaps"[14] was how Mum had
described the woods in BC's Coast Mountains. The coastal temperate
rainforest woke me up, too.

Next summer I was arrested with about sixty others for blocking
logging activity in Clayoquot Sound. (This was a year before the 932
arrests of 1993.) I was sentenced to house arrest, which meant I had
to secure a home immediately. It was time to settle down at last—a
thought that made me squirm. Vancouver Island's west coast is wild,
arguably romantic, but never quaint. Was this where I was supposed
to be? Furthermore, taking root meant no more fleeing. The annual
childhood trips to Mayne Island were made in flight from city life;
my trip to an idealized UK was a further flight from the past, and
even my trip back to Canada was in reaction to the pain of a break-
up. Settling down could only imply facing, rather than packing, my
baggage.

It wasn't easy to become a permanent fixture in a town rebuilt
for the wealthy. Moreover, while there were bitter feelings between

---

13   Pat Lowther, "On Reading a Poem Written in Adolescence," in *This Difficult Flowring* (Vancouver, BC:
Very Stone House, 1968). Recently published in *The Collected Works of Pat Lowther*, ed. Christine Wiesenthal.
14   Pat Lowther, "Coast Range," in *The Collected Works of Pat Lowther*, ed. Christine Wiesenthal.

Tofino and the logging town of Ucluelet to the south, Tofino also suffers polarization within its own boundaries. All this because of trees. Innocent, oblivious, ultra-political trees. I had made enemies before spending a single night in my new hometown.

> Trees are
> in their roots and branches,
> their intricacies,
> what we are
>
> ambassadors between the land
> and high air
> setting a breathing shape
> against the sky
> as you and I do
>
> ...
>
> Trees moving against the air
> diagram what is
> most alive in us ...[15]

My partner and I shared a house with several roommates for six months, knowing that we would have to move in the spring when bed and breakfast season resumed. Miraculously we were offered a log cabin five minutes from town, on the corner of sixteen-hectare Stockham Island. Out the back bear-proof door stood giant old-growth cedars, hemlock and Sitka spruce. In front spanned an unheard-of view: a multi-peaked mountain draped in uncut original rainforest. Mount Colnett's

---

15   Pat Lowther, "At the last judgment we shall all be trees" in *Milk Stone*. Recently published in *The Collected Works of Pat Lowther*, ed. Christine Wiesenthal.

flanks swept down to the prime bird habitat of Lemmens Inlet's mud-flats; all of this was Meares, the lopsided horseshoe-shaped island embracing all with its many thousands of hectares. Our cabin itself smelled like Sleepy Hollow, and I was happy to reacquaint myself with the peaceful absence of refrigerator hum. It was as easy as it was necessary to meditate on the front deck each morning before heading into town to work in a busy whale-watch booking office. My partner, Warren—whom I'd met on the Walbran blockade—hooked my laptop up to a solar panel. This way I was able to write when I was not splitting wood, heating rainwater or making compost.

Five years later the land was sold and we were evicted. The village had become even worse for average-income tenants. Warren had a windowless office in a basement suite with roommates downtown where we could sleep on the floor when necessary, but it was a bit cramped. On one of my last precious days at the cabin, I looked out the window and saw a floathouse being towed past. I had never seen or heard of floathouses before coming to Clayoquot Sound. Others were romanced by the very idea of such a life, but for someone who likes to step out her door and keep walking until she is good and ready to turn around, a floathouse seemed an unlikely home—an entrapment, even. But this one—a blue, barn-shaped cabin slowly sailing by—was just cute.

Warren came home later and mentioned that he had seen a poster about a floathouse for sale. He knew all about my fear of a sedentary existence enforced by an oceanic moat, the nearest shore impenetrable bush, and no other dwelling in sight. But I told him about the blue house on its way up the inlet. He said, "The one on the poster was blue."

We soon went to see it, parked just around a little peninsula from fellow activist Mike Mullin's own float—within swimming distance, yet out of sight. There was a creek for water. It seemed fated. Warren bought the place for $7,000: rare affordable housing, but most of the expense was yet to come. It was, after all, a couple of decades old.

I soon learned that my new life would be anything but sedentary, although it was rooted—anchored. Together, the wind and sea would rock us to sleep after long days of fixing up the place. Every moment floating would become precious.

Before we even began to unpack, though, I put up the hummingbird feeders. An immature rufous hummingbird joined a feisty troop of females, its beak much shorter than the adults'. Mature hummers zoomed up and surprised us; the juvenile took more time, approaching in a sort of aerial waddle, backside swaying under tentative wings. Sometimes it would perch on the flower it was feeding from and forget to fold its still-outstretched wings. This young bird knew what it had to do and was determined to practise and succeed, because survival depended on it. Consequently it was not as concerned with its surroundings as the adults were and would come quite close to us in pursuit of sustenance.

It often perched on the clothesline, wobbly, plump and downy, looking at the flowers, ignoring us, opening its beak to peep like a nestling. Was its mother among the adults?

The others abandoned their combative conduct at the feeder to give it a wide berth, and it perched at one of the four plastic yellow flowers. The most obnoxious bird (named "Rammer" by me) stationed itself on the line and drove everyone else off. Oblivious to the noisy clashes all around, the baby buried its bill in the plastic flower, its entire body rhythmically guzzling sugar water. When Rammer finally lost patience with Baby, the little one retreated to the line and peeped pitifully, its bill opened extraordinarily wide. Warren was eating a slice of watermelon, and Baby wobbled down to try a lick of that. It tried a nostril, too, with near disastrous results.

⤳

It was Warren's idea to add a second floating deck for a greenhouse garden, built by Stuart Crose and Joe Martin, and it was Warren's idea to ask woodwizard Robinson Cook to build a little solar-heated hot tub. The summer sun heats a large "collector" panel that warms the water. If the sky is cloudy, there's no bath. The greenhouse grows greens, tomatoes, potatoes, cukes, herbs. I try to feel the peace here between work shifts in town at various jobs, read a lot and try to write. Gardening can be hard work but it is sane abundance. Tofino's abundance leans in another direction: uncurbed growth measured in metres of parking and the square feet of mansions and condos. There is less habitat each year for wildlife, wolves are shot for preying on pets, people leave their garbage out; bears are attracted, become a threat to humans and are "destroyed." There is even a proposal to expand the airport by felling trees inside the national park.

The inlet's contrasting slow, tidal pace seeps into my bones, soothing. Friends visit from cities, enter Gratitude's parallel reality and find themselves sleeping more and better than they have for years. A harbour seal and a river otter sometimes share the space under the deck; eagles and kingfishers catch fish outside the window. A great blue heron lands on the dock, glares with its deadly, perfectly round eyes and deposits its white splat-signature. Writer Sy Montgomery spent quality time with emus in Australia. "Staring into that intelligent, shining brown eye," she confessed, "I felt as if I were capable of looking directly into the sun."[16]

With water, however, come movement and unrest. The horror of sinking lives in the back of my mind. After one November storm, my position turned ninety degrees overnight; two kayaks went up the creek, two panels (including the hot tub's) landed in the chuck, and the micro-hydro generator was dragged and damaged.

---

16   Sy Montgomery, "The Emus," in *The Nature of Nature: New Essays from America's Finest Writers on Nature*, ed. William H. Shore (San Diego: Harcourt Brace, 1994).

In summer, the horseflies can be particularly bad. Yet I find the hardest thing to bear is the sense of invasion when sailboats or yachts anchor a stone's throw away in a sound full of equally beautiful locations. When tourists paddle their dinghy around my cabin, staring through the windows, my own anger disturbs me.

I have lived fifteen years on the water, twenty-two years in Clayoquot Sound altogether. Warren and I are still friends and he is the precious handyman, visiting frequently. Housing in Tofino remains difficult, and groceries are expensive too. Most of the condos are vacation rentals, the mansions empty most of the year. Floating was rent-free, enabling me to survive, but now the BC government charges water dwellers a tax called a trespass fine—retroactively. Even so my gratitude grows deeper every year. Dragonflies mate in the air, slotted together, spiralling down like doomed airplanes. Bees bend back their hind legs to groom their wings. Moon jellies, during their annual reunion, join together in one long mass between the house and the dock; I can run my hand across the gelatinous, slippery surface. While I am swimming it is impossible to avoid colliding with dozens of them, but they don't sting. It rains more than three metres annually here, but sometimes when I think rain has come, dimpling the water from shore all the way to the farm, it's the moon jellies pulsating, tasting the air on a fragment of exposed flesh.

One autumn day a family of five river otters was feasting on perch, flicking their tails as they dove, sending up bubbles, and popping up with the shiny, wriggling fish. This went on for an hour, leading me to believe the bay must contain thousands of perch. When two smaller otters approached the float, I took up position bent over a gap in the planks on deck. Sure enough they were swimming close to the surface, around and past our flotation logs, just under the gap. One young whiskered face emerged between the water and me, and I said softly, "Hi." It disappeared and returned with its sibling; the two of them looked up at me for several seconds. After that there was a great deal of conversation between family members out of sight, as well as the usual din of crunching and lip-smacking—river otters have no table manners whatsoever. They were obviously curious animals, because one emerged onto the dock, looking cautiously around for me. I froze. Not seeing me behind the container garden, it dove. All was quiet, and I went indoors.

About a quarter of an hour later I glanced up from my window-side table. The whole family was dog-paddling steadily toward the house, five heads held high above the water, a live crab in every mouth.

At six feet from the dock they dove. Under the greenhouse deck, they feasted with audible gusto.

Another time, as I sat on the deck one spring afternoon, a lone river otter bubbled up from the deep and drew breath. Swallowing some morsel, she clambered onto the dock, shook herself and rolled on the warm, dry wood. Then she jumped to her feet and chewed her bum like a dog with fleas. She either didn't know I was sitting beside and slightly above her, or she didn't care as long as I remained still. I barely breathed. She used one foot to scratch her head, while the other pointed straight up, like a cat's. I could see the webbing between each clawed toe. Stretching her neck, she sniffed one of my potted tulips with her huge nostrils until a sigh of wind in the chimes startled her. Soundlessly, she slipped into her second skin—the ocean.

In his essay "Voyageurs," in *The Nature of Nature*, Scott Russell Sanders watches river otters playing and finds he wants things from them. "I wanted their company. I desired their instruction, as if, by watching them, I might learn to belong somewhere as they so thoroughly belonged here. I yearned to slip out of my skin and into theirs ..." He goes further, saying he wants from the otters the same thing he desires from everyone—friends, strangers, neighbours, his grown daughter:

I wanted their blessing. I wanted to dwell alongside them with understanding and grace. I wanted them to acknowledge my presence and go about their lives as though I were kin to them, no matter how much I might differ from them outwardly.[17]

His words express my own yearnings. For several days after the single otter's visit I kept waking up at 4:00 a.m. hearing splashes around the rocky shoreline. The fourth night of this, I propped myself up on an elbow and looked blindly out into the darkness, longing for some sort of visitation. I spotted something ghostly: bioluminescence around an animal moving swiftly toward the floathouse. As it dove, a thin coating of the submarine blanket of white light covered the body and I could see her—an otter—darting underwater hither and thither, a pale phantom. She finally scooted under the dock, leaving an explosion of white-green marine fireworks in her wake.

Wild creatures can seem like miracles, even aliens—like the screech owl that collided with my window and flapped hastily away, leaving its mouse dinner behind. Or the frog that swam, unfolding itself underwater into some long, thin creature I'd never known, and climbed out onto my foot. A swimming snake, a shimmering school of herring or a fluttering sphinx moth with extended proboscis can send me into raptures. Every time writer Natalie Angier sees a creature flash across her path unexpectedly, she describes it as being "more exhilarating than catching a glimpse of Al Pacino or Mikhail Baryshnikov on the streets of Manhattan."[18] For her, it's "a momentary state of grace." For Sy Montgomery, even when the emus she was studying became familiar, she fell in love with them:

---

17 Scott Russell Sanders, "Voyageurs," in *The Nature of Nature*, ed. William H. Shore.

18 Natalie Angier, "Natural Disasters," in *The Nature of Nature*, ed. William H. Shore.

It was raining harder, with a cold, bone-chilling wind. My coat and hair were drenched. I didn't care. I wanted only to find them … I realized that it wasn't the data I was after. I just wanted to be with them.[19]

Our own desires are clear; what of their effects? When does whale watching become whale chasing or bear watching become bear scaring? Wild animals neither want nor need my company. I have no wish to become the invader. At low tide I marvel at beings that, as far as I know, have no idea that I exist: sunstars, bat stars, pipefish (a cousin to the sea horse), slender kelp crabs and graceful dendronotids. All of these creatures thrive in the vulnerable marine eelgrass ecosystem. The best that I can hope for is undisturbed, undetected observation along with infrequent benevolent encounters, even though I yearn for a much deeper connection, even communion.

Only with humility is it possible to wake up to this place and its power. Every window open, I stretch out in the hammock, lullabied by varied thrushes and Swainson's thrushes. I have always found the spiralling song of the shy Swainson's thrush the most haunting of all birdsong.

In my semi-conscious state, their utterings are the voice of the forest. They come from all sides, a constant calling and answering, ricocheting around the bay. The level whistle of the varieds offers a sweet accompanying undertone.

Instantly all is silent. From the southeast shore a lone, sad howl issues forth into the still air. And again. No more.

The thrushes tentatively renew their calls, their spirals dizzying me toward slumber. I fancy there are bears huffing and rummaging among the rocks. I dream that my eyes are too heavy to open, so I can only listen. Gradually the voices of the birds grow strange, slow down,

---

19   Sy Montgomery, "The Emus," in *The Nature of Nature*, ed. William H. Shore.

deepen, birth an echo. Though I cannot see them through my paralyzed eyelids, I feel sure the bears are standing up on two legs and their attention is on the floathouse—on me. Goosebumps spread over my skin, like a school of fish suddenly brushing the water's surface as an eagle glides over. The beings on shore are people, or spirits. But they have no message for me. On the contrary, they are asking me something.

I wake up smartly then. There is only one thrush calling now, from a distance. I am overwhelmed by the dream, which is giving rise to new questions.

What is this place? The entire island is special enough to be a tribal park, so it would make sense if some of its bays, inlets or creeks were considered sacred to the Tla-o-qui-aht people. What about Gratitude's particular bay? Am I trespassing in a holy place? Something is creeping in, seizing my insides, rare, vital, not only Carr's "burning green in every leaf:"[20] every leaf, needle and cone has eyes. The air itself hums with alertness. Here is a glimpse into a patient, evolved dimension, more real and crucial than great cities. If the creek were ever to dry up, the sound of its silence would end the world. The forest watches warily, for Lone Cone must always continue talking "with casual / tongues of water / rising in trees,"[21] as my mother put it. Though I have not yet had visions, I have heard things.

My neighbour Mike, working on his oysters in a gale, watched helplessly as a Tasmanian-devilish waterspout spun toward him. The spout veered off at the last second, and as Mike gasped he inhaled a small rainbow. He says he's been happy ever since.

The future is unknowable; we can only breathe in the wonder that is this place now. My mother funnelled it into poems: "Look, we're riding past Venus"[22]

---

20   Emily Carr, *Growing Pains: The Autobiography of Emily Carr* (Douglas & McIntyre, 2005).

21   Pat Lowther, "Coast Range," in *The Collected Works of Pat Lowther*, ed. Christine Wiesenthal.

22   Pat Lowther, "Riding Past," in *Time Capsule* (Polestar Press).

She acknowledged her own desire to be

> aware of the spaces
> between stars, to breathe
> continuously the sources of sky,
> a veined sail moving,[23]

while she celebrated that

> The land is what's left
> after the failure
> of every kind of metaphor.[24]

I didn't know my mother wanted to live on a houseboat until after I was living on one myself. And how goosepimply was that little nugget of information, acquired from someone outside the family? Apparently, Mum fantasized about life upon the water because she thought it would require less housework, presumably due to a floathome's small size. She had laughingly reckoned a "houseboat" was something even a domestically challenged poet could manage. There would have been time to ponder sea anemones opening "their velvet bodies / … as huge / and glimmering / as flesh chandeliers."[25] Unlike Gratitude's relatively remote setting, I know she would have preferred to anchor hers in or near Vancouver waters and remain connected to the urban literary scene. But surely she would have loved this life, a cabin on the sea. Perhaps more poems about hermit crabs, anemones and jellyfish would have followed.

---

23   Pat Lowther, "Random Interview," in *Time Capsule*. Recently published in *The Collected Works of Pat Lowther*, ed. Christine Wiesenthal.
24   Pat Lowther, "Coast Range," in *The Collected Works of Pat Lowther*, ed. Christine Wiesenthal.
25   Pat Lowther, "Anemones," in *A Stone Diary*.

Growing up, I blundered my way out of despair by seizing words—my mother's, my own and many others'—and by pondering the ineffable stars. So far I haven't succeeded in growing armour on my freckled hide and, anyway, even the toughest bark gets scorched. I revel in the electric chill of the astringent ocean on my skin. At home in Gratitude, sensitivity is a gift, the preferred state of mind. In the meantime, there is much work to do and it's important to find strength. Clearcutting continues, moving into some of the planet's last pristine valleys. We toiled to save a single tree in Tofino and were forced to wrap it in steel to make it "safe" for vacation condominiums below. The world craves sanity. I am grateful for sanctuary.

COME OVER TO THE DARK SIDE

Pity the dark: we're so concerned to overcome and banish it,
it's crammed full of all that's devilish, like some grim cupboard
under the stair.

—Kathleen Jamie, *Findings*

Even though everybody knows it's darkness that makes us appreciate the light, the dark gets a pretty bad rap.

"There are dark times ahead."

"These are dark days." (Never said with excitement or a smile.)

Dark equals bad. Dark equals evil. In North American culture "light is idealized and dark is devalued" even while "seeds are planted underground, the womb is dark, and life forms itself anew in hidden places."[26] I'm quoting *Dreaming the Dark* by Miriam Simos, more widely known as Starhawk—a practitioner of Wicca. James Sharpe's 1996 book on witches and witchcraft in England from 1550 to 1750 is titled *Instruments of Darkness*. Despite having written a meticulous volume, Sharpe resorted to the old cliché with his title.

I like the dark time. There is nothing better than a fully waned moon in the month of November, when I was born. Scorpio: brooding, tempestuous, unpredictable, intense, dramatic. I am referring of course to the weather, not my personality. Driveways disappear under slippery layers of brown alder leaves. Parts of the world become hidden.

---

26   Miriam Simos, *Dreaming the Dark: Magic, Sex, and Politics* (Boston: Beacon Press, 1982).

In Canada's temperate zone—the west coast—it rains a lot, the sky is often grey and snow is scarce. There are locals here who suffer from seasonal affective disorder, or SAD, a depression caused by short, dark days. I often wonder why these sufferers chose to live here, and why they choose to stay. We can have weeks on end without the tiniest hint of blue sky. Everybody's stumbling around as if they are inside the murkiest Emily Carr painting.

I also suffer from SAD—in summer. I call it summer-alienation dysfunction. At the troublesome age of thirteen, long before the invention of the internet, I lived in a group home for a year. During the long, hot, endlessly sunny summer, there was virtually nothing to do. I seemed to have no friends and was out of touch with my family, and the other girls who lived there were away most of the time. Many of my days were spent writing unbelievably depressing drivel. Ever since that year, I cannot abide working indoors if the weather is fair. I seek adventure, hiking or kayaking but generally end up alternating between gardening obsessively and jumping in the ocean. Long days, brief nights and lengthy bouts of sunshine find me wilting and searching for large rocks under which to crawl, or caves with their comforting drip, drip to remind me of the dark times. Because usually, during Scorpio and on into the winter, darkness equals rain.

A really good rain washes the world. It feeds and quenches the forest. It helps the salmon get up the rivers to spawn. Our rain makes us the envy of much of the rest of the planet. Before learning from water activist Maude Barlow about the "myth of abundance" and the threat of corporate control of H_2O, I often wondered why we didn't capture Vancouver Island rain in big barrels and ship it to Africa.[27] What is it like to be so thirsty you have to suck leaves? I watch miniature streams run down paved streets, no use to anyone, but beautiful

27   *Water on the Table*, dir. Liz Marshall (Toronto: LizMars Productions, 2010).

the way art is beautiful, curving in random patterns, dimpled by falling drops. It seems so bountiful.

I've never danced naked in the rain—at least, not that I can remember. A romantic idea, probably a summer activity. It's good when it rains in summer. You might think everyone would like the combination of warm and wet, but they don't, so I try to look sympathetic while others complain. But there is too much daylight for my taste.

I get excited at the approach of Hallowe'en, the old pagan new year. All Hallow's Eve is when the veil between the worlds of life and death is thinnest and we can honour and receive guidance from those who have passed over. A clear night for trick-or-treaters is welcome, but it's even better if the rain starts pouring down just after the last group of children is home safe. All Hallow's marks the beginning of peak Scorpio storm time. Mystery: we cannot control the elements. Music: wind fussing the trees and hail drumming the roof. Literature: cozying up to a good book next to the fire.

Let us reclaim "dark times ahead" as a positive statement, welcoming the new year, the oncoming winter, and the Reign of Night. Pete Townshend of the Who once sang, "and the night comes down like a cell door closing."[28] But I think the night moves in soothing and safe, obliterating the glaring light and petty annoyances of the day. No longer exposed, you relax as the darkness and weather seep into your bones like a particularly effective massage oil. Seek solace in the womblike darkness. Go back to the source. Be inspired by the power.

An especially ferocious storm means power outages, a misnomer. Lighting candles, stoking the woodstove, you peer out the window to witness true, bristling, planetary power, raw and chaotic. Have you ever been outside at night during gale-force winds, looking across a body of water at the twinkling lights of a distant community, when

---

28 Pete Townshend, "However Much I Booze," *The Who by Numbers*, MCA, 1975.

the electricity goes out? Poof! No lights, no community. You are filled with an unexpected reverence. A humless quiet descends, and over the wind the loud cries of black turnstones fill your ears, which you didn't even notice a moment ago. Now you realize the well-camouflaged shorebirds must be foraging on the rocks just below where you stand. How long have they been there? The salty smell of eelgrass and mud reaches your nostrils; there are fewer distractions to your ears and eyes in the starless dark, and all the senses benefit. You detect a slight rustling vibration in the air close by—in fact, from the top of the tree next to you; a heron erupts with ghastly, commanding squawks and opens its huge, cupped wings to depart. You can't see this. But you feel it. You can hear coons or minks quarrelling on the rocks, probably frightening the turnstones away. Or maybe this new sound is river otters, mating. The new, deeper darkness brings the night to life.

These creatures are grateful for the night, and they cope well with storms. They don't need a roof over their heads. I imagine homeless humans dealing with short days, storms, relentless rain. If I were one of them, my feelings might change. Drastically. Shivering in my cardboard box or leaky tent, I'd pray for stars. I'd pray for merciful sunshine, and sense deep relief when the nights began to shorten again. I know this is true. Nevertheless, the dark would still be my ally, hiding me in its mother-cloak from pitying, disapproving eyes.

In Pursuit

Pre-encounter

O elusive one, o ultimate wildness, I must have proof of this magic,
I must witness you: the forest breathing, alive, flicking its tail.

Since 1992 I have lived in Clayoquot Sound. Wolves and black bears
are at home in this habitat, which happens also to be one of the most
cougar-populated ecosystems in the world. Yet chance sightings of the
great cat are extremely rare.

The forests here contain immense western red cedars, some believed to be as old as two thousand years, alongside Sitka spruce and
hemlock just as wise. Heavy clumps and mattresses of moss grow on
strong branches. In the dark and tangled understorey of broad-leaved
evergreen salal, huckleberry, thorny salmonberry and myriad ferns,
legendary megafauna like cougars are born and live out their lives.

This magnificent predator is so elusive that any sight of one is likely
to be on the animal's terms—and likely the last thing you will ever see.
I once asked a native man from the Tla-o-qui-aht nation why there are
almost no representations of cougars created by his people's artists. He
told me that to even speak of the cougar is taboo. It is the most serious
danger of the land. I began to sense that catching sight of one and living to remember it would be miraculous. "Some of us admire the skill
of a creature in travelling unseen and in living among human residents
undetected,"[29] wrote Gary Thorp in *Caught in Fading Light: Mountain*

---

29   Gary Thorp, *Caught in Fading Light: Mountain Lions, Zen Masters, and Wild Nature* (New York: Walker &
Company, 2002).

Lions, Zen Masters, and Wild Nature. These silent predators blend in with their surroundings and are masters at legerdemain, so that seeing them is indeed catching them, if only for a moment. Magic intrigues.

But it was neither magic nor the taming of capture that I sought a few years after I'd moved to the coast. Like Thorp, safely sighting a cougar became a new goal for me. I cherished my feeling of closeness to the forest, wrote poetry about moving slowly and deliberately as banana slugs in narrow, moist corners, comforted by an autumn day's dark. I longed for secrets this place might willingly share with me, pieces of its deepest, truest wildness. To witness the forest breathing, alive, flicking its tail.

Some people said I might as well be asking to see a sasquatch. And I was *asking* to see a cougar: making a request, not a demand. Yet I wasn't thinking about this on my way to a children's camp behind Catface Mountain.

The year was 1996, still summer, a mere two weeks after I had firmly made my resolution. Catface is named for its two peaks resembling a cat's ears, which are currently under threat from copper mining. Catface's southern beach supports a few off-grid cabins but no village. All of it—slope, sand, rocky shoreline—is dominated by rainforest.

The volunteer-run camp was held behind the mountain at Whitepine Cove, an uninhabited traditional territory (called IR, for Indian Reserve, on official maps) across Herbert Inlet and Calmus Passage from the Native village of Ahousat. A well-meaning local wanted to mimic the popular Rediscovery camps, whose mandate is "Drawing on the teachings of Indigenous peoples and the wisdom of the Elders, with a philosophy of love and respect for each other and the earth, Rediscovery seeks to empower youth of all ages to discover the world within themselves, the world between cultures and the natural world."[30]

---

30   Rediscovery International Foundation, "Our Philosophy," Rediscovery.org, http://rediscovery.org (accessed July 22, 2014).

Disembarking from the delivery boat, I could see how informal, even disorganized, this imitation camp was. Children ran free, unwatched. A litter of refuse and toys lay scattered across the grass and sand; remains of food and dirty dishes sat unattended. Unburied human scats decorated the high-tide line, and the privy was a rank hole in the ground with a bag of lime next to it at the forest's edge.

Fortunately, there were other, better scents in the air as well. Well away from the dung, Tla-o-qui-aht Billie Martin was making chowder with clams he had dug from the sand ten minutes earlier. I soon worried that bears would be attracted by our smorgasbord of ripe aromas. Indeed, glancing up from the hunk of bannock I was frying, I noticed one on the other side of the bay, looking our way and sniffing the air with its black snout. Luckily, as someone shook out a roll of tarp, the bear fled the unfamiliar sound.

Encounter

O surprising one, both longed for and unexpected, the imagined has been delivered even to the shaky ground where I stand.

At 4:00 p.m. I headed for the privy, preparing to hold my breath. Before turning the last corner into the trees, I paused and called out, "Anybody using the toilet?" And around the corner came a cougar.

We both stopped. I know it's a cliché, but my world shuddered into slow motion. Shadows flickered across the tan-coloured body; the tail twitched; the head looked away and back. The eyes remained obscured in the shade. The creature hesitated ... turned ... vanished.

A period of slow disbelief ensued. Was there a dog in camp I hadn't noticed all day? I had to know. Children's lives were suddenly at stake. I sprinted after the animal.

Behind the privy it stood, flanked by salmonberry bushes, salal, young alders and one scruffy yew. Its back to me, the cat-face turned again, eyes still in shadow. If my own eyes doubted, my ears confirmed the truth. The cougar meowed sweetly once and vanished again. I stood there vibrating in shock at the sound, my ears and feet humming. What to do now? Where would it go next? With its mild, innocent call tingling in my eardrums, I forced myself into further action.

Post-encounter

O silent one, o ghostly danger, though you are nowhere to be seen,
I feel you, I know you now to be everywhere.

Hurrying back to camp, I yelled, "Cougar! Cougar!" Everyone stared, but there was no panic. One girl mock-screamed; a few of the kids laughed. Another adult volunteer ran down to the privy and returned breathless with confirmation: she had seen the tawny rear end and tail of the cat slipping into the bush.

We rounded everybody up and moved all the tents into a tight circle. I don't remember if we were unable to reach Ahousat by radio or if no boats were available; in any case, we could not leave until the following day. I lay in my tent that night, astonished, my mind looping through known facts versus new data. A ferocious wild beast, *meow?* They are known to scream, hiss, growl, utter bloodcurdling mating calls, emit a "silent snarl," even whistle and chuckle. I knew it was extremely fortunate that the cougar had met me rather than a small child. Had I experienced a *friendly* cougar encounter?

We packed up next morning in time for our scheduled Ahousat boat and departed. The cove slowly withdrew from sight.

In town, it was frustrating to see doubt and outright disbelief on people's faces when I told them a cougar meowed at me. When I telephoned my urbanite sister, however, she believed me immediately.

"I've seen lots of wildlife documentaries," she said. "Mother cougars meow to their young, so why not?"

Then I called local conservation officer Bob Hansen. He explained that young cougars are known for their curiosity, and learn through trial and error. Sometimes they are looking for their mothers, who abandon them abruptly after up to eighteen months together. Sub-adults have been known to follow people for several kilometres. Perhaps "my" cougar had been inexperienced, testing the context of our meeting, assessing the situation this way: "Are you prey? Why aren't you cowering or running? I'm confused. I think I'll go now ..." The meow *had* felt like a question.

I wished I had seen its eyes. We were right there, cat-face to human-face; had I in fact seen them and somehow blocked the memory? The cat may have preferred to keep its highly sensitive pupils shaded. What also continues to haunt me after all these years is that this predator, friendly as it seemed, was in front of me with no warning. Its feet made no sound: not in approach, not in retreat.

The cougar had moved like a ghost, had come out of nowhere: a forest, which to me used to be everywhere, home, a place where I went to be alone and comforted "in narrow, moist corners."[31] I had lived for many years in a log cabin, hunted wild mushrooms in the forest outside my door, written a book of poems about being healed by forests; I had even been arrested trying to protect forests from clearcut logging. But post-cougar poems were sobered by the green wall of wildness I look at from my floathouse surrounded by water—a moat protecting me from the forest. I am no longer comfortable venturing ashore, much less hiking into the trees. Not alone, anyway. I found myself writing:

---

31 Christine Lowther, "Mushroom Dreamtime," in *My Nature* (Lantzville, BC: Leaf Press, 2010).

Do not allow your kayak to drift
close to shore

...

A cougar could drop
from the wall and pin you,
your paddle spinning away like
an ungainly oak seed,
sink fangs into your neck
drag you over the shredding rocks
force you through the wall
into darkness.[32]

On a July morning in 2010, I was sitting on my creekside deck at low tide. Just as I was thinking of heading inside to escape the brisk wind, three wolves—two grey, one black—emerged from the trees, trekked past (pointedly ignoring me) along the rocks, and re-entered the forest.

That familiar stunned sensation returned, abruptly. Yes, I always knew forests were megafauna territory, yet when the cougar—and fourteen years later, the wolves—materialized, I was shocked. How I once felt about the forest is forever changed; there is fear now. Through the porous wall of wildness I could become prey, so I keep within my solid walls of shelter. Though I will always fight for the forest, I am not ready for that form of belonging: death, which makes equals of all in nature, the brilliant humans sustenance for centipedes. Wild predators and people belong together in death, belong *to* death, that last wall. Killed by a cougar ... an honourable way to go. A fair and natural way to go.

---

32 Christine Lowther, "Wall of Wild," in *My Nature*.

I made a pact with fate, was granted my wish and shaken by my own fragility. Facing the friendly beast was, in fact, facing death. No wonder that people are afraid of the forest, that the first settlers, fighting for survival, made it their first priority to tame the wild. Today I know I could find happiness, even bliss, in passing through the green wall regularly and often, to a place that can teach profound humility. But I also sympathize with the view that some places should be left to their non-human inhabitants. To belong does not necessarily mean to be safe; every non-human being knows this.

This past autumn I saw a cougar bounding away from the car I was riding in. Rather than fresh encounters, now all I request is courage. And I wonder. What did our meeting mean to the cougar? Did the animal carry me as a lifelong memory? Me, in pursuit, held in the mind of a great wild cat, deep in the rainforest.

> Now all I hunt is the peace
> that is lost to me,
> and I cannot blame you
> who offered yourself—
> innocence, might, and grace—
> to something unbelievably fragile, tame.[33]

---

[33] Christine Lowther, "To the Mountain Lion That Opened its Lips and Spoke to Me." Previously unpublished.

Attack Of The Killer Pink Sea Star

Starfish scare me. Enough to cause me to go to the trouble of calling them by their proper name: sea stars—phylum Echinodermata. Sounds beautiful, but I know too much. For a start, sea stars are of the class Asteroidea, which raises the question, do they even belong here on Earth?

Consider some of their behaviours. Mud stars eat mud; rose stars, which bristle with what might as well be thorns, dine on their own cousins and sea slugs. Yes, sea stars are deadly predators, and besides that, some of them clearly look like unhinged aliens.[34] Would you want to meet the likes of a fat blood star in *your* dreams?

Perhaps you like the look of a cookie star? Eating one would poison you.

Think the cushion star looks squeezable and comfortable? It will smother for food.

Find nothing macabre about the beautiful morning sun star? It eats other sea stars, with a marked preference to its cousin (non-morning) sun stars. It will even cannibalize its own kind.

A fleshy wrinkled star will grasp one end of a rock, looking for all the world like a disembodied human hand. A spiny red star will impale soft fingers. The swollen-looking gunpowder star smells strongly like exploded gunpowder, and has been found "humped up

---

34   Philip Lambert, *Sea Stars of British Columbia, Southeast Alaska and Puget Sound* (Victoria, BC: Royal British Columbia Museum, 2000).

over clusters of fringed filament-worms"[35] like a Klingon enjoying *gagh*. The slimy-surfaced leather star has an unexpected garlic-like aroma, and bat stars, otherwise known as webbed stars, ooze dissolving digestive juices over prey. Indeed, like a fast-food-addicted North American, bat stars extend their stomachs over myriad animals and plants.

Foragers of live or dead animals (they're not bothered which), sea stars have more arms and more cleavage than we'll ever have. And they move fast. Sunflower stars grow from five-armed juveniles to twenty-four-armed adults measuring eighty centimetres in diametre. These are the fastest of all the stars: one was clocked at 115 centimetres per minute. Do not underestimate the power. Sunflower stars, while initially recalling those beautiful symbols of summer, are equipped with fifteen thousand tube feet and can capture—and *swallow*—anything from Dungeness crabs to heavily armed sea urchins. (If I were a sea urchin I'd rather be eaten by a cute, cuddly sea otter.) Some sea stars can even snare certain kinds of bottom fish. So it's not only the immobile or slow prey for them.

In a truly horrific way, moon snails also come into this. Tourists love moon snail shells—their smooth, classic turban shape, their subtle colours—and are astonished to learn that they are native to Clayoquot Sound, and aren't some exotic import. In local stores, moon snail shells are fashioned into coloured candle holders and rattles. Little do admirers know that these animals drill a hole in every sand dollar they can find and suck the flesh out. When they get tired, they suffocate the dollars with their one huge, slimy foot. (Sand dollars cost two dollars plus tax in the town of Tofino.)

As horrible as the moon snails are, it is a terrible sight to behold a sunflower star attacking one (especially if the snail is in the middle of

---

35   Neil McDaniel, "Gunpowder Star," *Sea Stars of the Pacific Northwest*, http://www.seastarsofthepacific-northwest.info/species/gunpowder_star.html (accessed July 22, 2014).

devouring something itself). But who can look away? Especially when you know the star's lower stomach is protruding through its mouth to envelope its prey and that the snail will spend several hours being digested inside it.

Here is what writer Briony Penn says of these stars:

> Sunflower stars are second only to Moon Snails for having the slimiest, weirdest bodies ever to inspire manufacturers of rubber gadgets ... reminiscent of something between the Slime Slurp and a *Star Wars* villain ... huge, slimy, rapid-moving stars, sometimes reaching a metre across, with as many as 25 legs that are mottled colours of purple, orange and greeny grey—an interior decorator's nightmare. They are also breeding down in the mud right now and you can see all their little darlings getting ready to grow and become the scourges of the mudflats.[36]

Penn dares us to get close to one of these animals "charging across" the mud "at a foot per second ... when the dinner bell is rung to devour a pound of snail."

If you happen to drop a pail of oysters overboard, do not bother diving down after them. It is too late. The well-armed rulers of the mud will already be converging on your succulent treat, covering the shells with their bodies, putting all those tube feet to work and prying open the helpless things. (Like you wanted to do.) Consider it an offering, but do not believe you can ever get on any sea star's good side. They probably remember all the times you have pried them off of rocks. They might want revenge.

---

36   Briony Penn, *A Year on the Wild Side* (Victoria: TouchWood Editions, 1997).

The only animal clever and quick enough to evade sea stars is the endangered abalone, beloved by jewellery lovers. This critter knows to speed away and swivel its shell violently to shake off the suckers of the deadly attacker posing innocently as a flower. (If you ask me, they look more like overgrown tarantulas.) Also worthy of mention is a small parasitic snail that heroically inserts its sucking mouth-parts through the body wall of any sea star, sucking out the internal fluids. Talk about David and Goliath.

I am afraid of the giant pink star most of all. No other five-armer in Clayoquot Sound can match it for size and bulk. Its colour? A sickly grey-pink. It competes with humans by eating clams, including the phallic geoducks. I catch myself visualizing it standing up and running on two of its limbs. Imagining it in my dreams: pasty as putty, tall as Joey Ramone, giving chase, waving its long arms maniacally.

LIVING LIGHT

"What on Earth is that noise?"

"More accurate to ask, 'What in the ocean?'"

"Well, what in the ocean, then?"

"That's my resident harbour seal."

"You're kidding!"

This was a conversation I had all last summer, whenever visitors came to my floating home. A young seal would often rest on one of the flotation logs under my greenhouse and snore. Sometimes it would blow bubbles in the lapping water, the sound alternating between peaceful, humorous and rude depending on the seal's whim.

The animal had not yet learned to be shy of humans; this much was evident in its relaxed, unafraid behaviour. Earlier in the season I had heard it crying for its mother over on the rocks beside the island flanking my neighbour's oyster farm. It was a plaintive sound, but I knew not to intervene. This was nature: the mother went fishing and the pup missed her. The baby was not abandoned. Many times I had heard of people picking up what they thought was an orphaned seal and taking it to a rescue centre—mistakenly causing the permanent separation between parent and offspring that they believed had already occurred. On the other hand, I also knew the odd sharp-eyed local who had rescued young seals at death's door.

I frequently got in my kayak and floated close enough to the rocks to spy on the pup through binoculars, making sure it was not in trouble.

But as long as it continued calling loudly like that, there was a good bet nothing was amiss. It still had strength. It wanted food.

Later, as the seal grew, it seemed to gain some independence and took my little bay for its own. It would surface to inspect whatever humans happened to be paddling around. In general, harbour seals like to follow me, always with a peaceful slow-breathing presence, patiently watching through those large, liquid eyes. One seal, two, sometimes even three, will tag along. They won't come as far as the main channel of Lemmens Inlet, where I venture to look for porpoises; other seals are already there. I am not expert enough to tell them apart. But I did get to know the one that took to swimming near my houseboat. He or she was small and lightly coloured compared to the other seals, and came closer. Much closer.

"No. I'm not kidding. Come see for yourself. You have to tiptoe."

The seal would be resting on a log a mere couple of inches from the floorboards of the greenhouse. A quiet person could lie down and place her eye to one of the gaps between the floorboards—and would have to hold her breath or the seal might feel it. I'd look down on the back of its grey head and watch the long whiskers around its nose and study the mottled pattern of its fur. I could hear every nuance of breath; a sudden snort could be startling.

There are, of course, many other animals in my world. I am anchored at an apex of freshwater stream, salt sea, and ancient temperate rainforest. This coming together of habitats teems with wildlife. Black bears wander the shoreline, turning over rocks. Minks emerge from the ocean, shake their gorgeous fur and scamper up the rocks into the forest. Raccoons dig in the early morning low-tide mud. Bald eagles teach their young to fish. Families of river otters help themselves to my decks, climbing aboard to roll on the warm wood and deposit their droppings. The babies unabashedly run over my solar panels. Otters have growled up at me from between the floorboards.

They eat lustily and noisily, crunching on shells and crabs. They are wild. Last summer's seal, I liked to tell myself, was not so wild. I pretended it was mine.

It might be closer to the mark to say I was the seal's pet human. I waited for him, looked for him. I thrilled with each sighting or encounter, marvelled over his graceful skill in the water, felt goosebumps when I knew I was being watched. I would look up to meet those huge eyes, calmly fixed on me from a position next to one of the landlines anchoring a corner of my home to the shore. For a moment, we would both just look.

"Hello there."

The seal would nonchalantly tip backwards to return to its submarine realm. I often saw him gliding close to the bottom, upside down, ignoring fishes, which appeared to tolerate the predator in their midst. A spidery slender kelp crab creeping along the submerged rope might catch my attention, and when my eyes flickered back, the seal would be gone.

Other times, at a distance, I would hear a telltale broadcast splash. It wasn't seals playing, or courting, or arguing. It was seals surrounding schools of fish and scaring hundreds out of the water at once, causing the sound of many small bodies slapping the surface as they fell back down to their doom, or their escape, as the case may be. This feeding technique could be a group effort or carried out by only one seal. Although it must have been terrifying for the fish, I always liked the sound—found it relaxing, even. I knew that seals, perhaps including my favourite one, were feasting. Splash after splash would fill the bay, sometimes with an echo off the side of Lone Cone. A skilled seal could keep the school in one spot. Less work. More eating.

I never got into the water when the seal was around. I had no wish to frighten this creature in his own habitat, his only home, and risk destroying our comfortable, convenient and (to me) deeply satisfying companionship. I had tried swimming with other seals in the past. They had come near enough to ascertain that I was something from which to flee, leaving me disappointed and alone in the cold briny water. No. I was determined not to scare my young friend. Yet for all I knew he was observing me the times I did take to the water. I cannot pretend to have known his whereabouts at all times.

Near the end of September it was time to make the most of the bioluminescence before the autumn storms began, darkening the water and forcing me indoors. Bioluminescence is, quite literally, living light. Dinoflagellates, single-celled plantlike organisms, produce flashes and submarine sparks through a chemical reaction when agitated. These light effects are pure magic, whether streaming from my paddle with every stroke or making the faster-swimming fish glow.

My friend Maryjka arrived for a sleepover one night. She came to kayak around the house under the stars—and to create galaxies of her own. While she paddled around the bay, I enjoyed the hot tub, as I did on many summer nights. That may sound opulent, but the tub is funky rather than classy, made from salvaged cedar. After a few sunny days the water gets surprisingly hot. So hot, in fact, that I take breaks by diving into the ocean, enveloping my body with white-green light.

"Do you think this totem animal of yours will make an appearance?" called Maryjka from the kayak.

"If so, you'll hear breathing close by," I answered from the tub.

The air was still, trillions of stars dominating the world. The Milky Way was huge, a swath of "biolume" curtaining the wide sky that spanned both decks.

Soaking away the weariness of peak-tourist-season servitude that bound me to Tofino, I became aware that Maryjka was speaking again. She sounded like she was talking to a baby. I sat up straight and listened more closely.

"Hello sweetie, how *are* you? Oh, so *nice* to hear you and to *see* your pretty, *pretty* lightshow!"

"Uh, Maryjka?"

"Oh, hello, *hello* sweetie!"

"Is it—?"

"It's the seal, look! It's surrounded by bioluminescence! It's like a white cloud circling the kayak!"

I had never heard her so excited.

"Come in closer," I demanded. She paddled gently up to the float. There. Something like Casper the Friendly Ghost, or a seal in photographic negative: silvery, ethereal, wrapped in a veil of living light. A frisky aura scooting around her boat. Then the water darkened. The seal had surfaced. We could hear it breathing between us. That close.

"I'm getting in," I said.

"*What?*"

As soon as the seal had submerged again, I clambered out of the tub, but instead of diving into the dark sea, I slowly lowered myself in, gripping the deck. The water was heart-stopping, as usual, a great contrast to the temperature of the hot tub. But I was used to going back and forth. I found it invigorating and even a little bit dangerous. And now I was going in with a seal.

Over the years, I have had eyebrows raised at my approach to wild animals. I swim with moon jellyfish. Why not? They don't sting. Once, onto a deck packed with gawking visitors, every swimming guest quickly vacated the ocean when a fourteen-legged, green, antennaed isopod torpedoed through the water. Me? I jumped in to check it out.

I know there are scores of people who travel vast distances and undergo various kinds of suffering to get close to wildlife. I'm not special. I have read about scientists falling in love with their research animals, ignoring extreme weather just to be near them, no longer collecting data. I don't suspect anthropomorphism. I think it is rather akin to fierce love, a longing that makes us reach from our limited, tame, human selves. We want to belong to a place in the way they do.

I did not have to wait long for the seal to come to me. Its stream-lined form circled and swished directly beneath me, just out of reach of my stretching toes. Maryjka sat speechless as I gasped with excitement. After a few moments, I felt contact. A quick, careful flipper grazed my heel. That was all, and that was enough.

ORIGIN OF A DREAMCATCHER

Tofino sprawls across its host, a slim peninsula. Summer brings a zoo of visitors, winter isolating tempests. Progress oozes along the highway between what can feel like two opposing oceans: open, rolling surf to the west, muddy slough to the east. The ooze appears to seep farther with every passing year. Even so, it seems there's always room for more high-priced developments while those who can't afford them scramble to find and hang on to affordable housing.

When I first moved to the floathouse in May 1998 I wasn't spooked by being off the grid or living five nautical miles away from noise and distraction, or even the anchor-dragging storms that threatened to hurl me and my house onto the rocks. It was the spectre of losing connection to terra firma, to wandering the trails every day without fear, my hands pausing to caress the fibrous bark of immense cedar trees.

Now I am afloat. Drifting in a kayak next to the house, looking at the trees instead of touching them. This forest is Meares Island, fifteen kilometres long and almost as wide. The only people living on the land are far away, on the Opitsaht Reserve, a tiny village across the harbour from Tofino. When I first moved onto the float, a long-time Clayoquot resident visited me and pointed vaguely toward the creek saying that a rough old wolf trail passed through a bog to a lake. If I were to leave my protective moat and explore that path, I would be the lone human.

"The shore is cougar territory," she added. "Respect that."

"You mean, don't hike alone?"

"Stay away."

For my first few years floating, time rolled on with evidence of neither wolves nor cougars. Still, I didn't dare explore. Black bears would sometimes patrol the shore, turning over rocks, grazing on the grass, cooling off in the water, swimming away—or, more often, re-entering the forest exactly where I believed the trail to be.

It is 2006: a dry year, which is easy living for me but will later throw Tofino and its tourist economy into mayhem. National news: the rainforest's first water shortage. My creek keeps flowing through the crisis. Note the human arrogance: *my* creek. *Our* water resources.

I seek shade, and the forest offers it. So I remind myself: the shore I'm anchored to is Meares Island, for heaven's sake. It was declared a tribal park by the Tla-o-qui-aht people after they stood in front of Mac-Millan Bloedel's chainsaws. They have not forsaken it. Why should I?

It takes only a few paddle strokes from the floathouse to reach land. I tie my kayak to a slim alder. The tide is still rising. A couple of ravens croak overhead as I clamber along rocks, tiptoeing around limpets and barnacles. Wild Nootka roses are blooming, and their scent leads me to the creek mouth. There, I have to grin at a piece of faded flagging tape hanging limply from a salal bush: the beginning of the trail. I've built this moment up in my mind as some kind of brave and mystical milestone, the long-awaited move from comfort and security into the maw of wildness, following the way of bears. Yet someone has put up flagging tape. Perhaps there will be boardwalk, too, and stairs with handrails? Circular decks around stately ancient hemlocks and Sitka spruce; interpretive signage every few metres.

Instead, I am bushwhacking through tangled salal, tripping over roots. The damp, cool smell of the creek permeates the close air.

Then, a wall of moss looms up beside me. Absurd clumps of the stuff interspersed with delicate deer ferns decorating a massive boulder left behind by the obligatory ice age. I always think of moss as green and damp. This is brown and dry, crisp and scratchy against my skin.

I look at the ground around my feet. Everybody's here: salmonberry, huckleberry, cynamocka, devil's club, swordfern, lady fern, licorice fern; soft baby salal leaves sprouting from robust, dark green precursors. I seek the oddballs, scouring the earth for pale Indian pipe and groundcone. My search brings me to the crest of a slight slope, where a screen of leaves veils the path. I remember reading somewhere about an American indigenous tribe said to have forty names for different parts of each leaf. Could I ever become so at home here? Wary of thorns, I carefully move the greenery aside, hoping this is the end of actual bushwhacking. The veil closes behind me. I can no longer hear the creek or the ravens. There is a deep silence. The creek's moist scent is gone and my nostrils contract. One step, and my sandals crunch on the dry ground, snapping everything underneath to bits. Tree trunks look more grey than they ought. Unfurling new ferns threaten to crumble. And it is not yet summer.

As I proceed cautiously in the midst of this aridity, miraculously, a bog begins underfoot. I begin to see skunk cabbages, scores of them, broad leaves and late, yellow-hooded spikes growing directly from the mud. But this is not postcard-pretty habitat. Bogs are not the lush dreamscapes of giant spruce. Lean, straight white pines do average thirty metres tall, but they are few and far between the dominant species: stunted shore pines. These dwarves are tangled with straggly, brittle debris, a dumpsite of elbows sticking out at crazy angles, spear-ended snags pointing sharply, stabbing at the unwary. While useless for fine woodwork, many pieces are beautiful in their uncanny, gnarled way. Though they're small, they are also old. Somehow the trees keep growing despite a lack of nutrients, a void caused by acid-releasing sphagnum moss. I try to avoid stepping on the stuff; I don't want to wreck the place.

This landscape of disorder is completely alien to what most people are used to, including me.

Apart from a sudden hummingbird fanning the parched air into a tremor of sound, I am making the only din in this world, mud sucking my sandals. I sense an awareness, nevertheless. I see no other life, but am myself being watched. When the drumming of a ruffed grouse's wings erupts as if from deep underground, a cry nearly escapes my lips. No doubt the bird merely seeks a mate, but this drumming is like the soil itself sending some coded message. I could let my imagination go. Fairies. Sasquatch. D'Sonoqua. Green Man. Ancestors. Ghosts.

A welcome distraction: western bog laurel blooms everywhere, gentle pink against the backdrop of scaly grey pine bark. Common butterwort, too, tiny and inconspicuous, yet royal purple and carnivorous to boot. Its only leaves lie in a rosette firmly against the ground, anchoring the plant. Starflowers appear next, but I'm on the hunt again, this time for red columbine. Distraction from the painfully obvious is welcome, for I am walking in generations of bears' footprints, their tracks permanently entrenched in the mudscape. Every now and again large holes full of water show me where bears have recently excavated skunk cabbages to feast on the roots. Many other prints in all sizes tell stories in the soft ground, but I cannot translate, only guess wildly: raccoon, squirrel, river otter, mink, wolf, cougar or the elusive marten. All I'm sure of is that bear and wolf prints will have claw marks above the toe pads, while cougar prints will not.

It has been decades since this land was under threat. Instead of columbine flowers, unlikely mineral-extraction claim posts materialize, two small metal signs nailed into stumps. "Lone Cone II, Locator Terry McCullough, July 13, 1972." The second one is dated 1987, quite long enough to have lapsed.

As I've been poring over the ground and watching closely where I place my filthy feet, the bog has given way to dense forest. The skunk cabbages have lost their declining blooms; they grow prehistoric-sized leaves. I leap over streams that gurgle several feet below their banks.

Abruptly, the forest ends and a meadow begins. I emerge again as if from a wall and must skirt the meadow or sink and lose my sandals—or worse. Maybe this is the proper bog; the ground is impassable. What happened to the bear trail? The sun is hot. I finally spot columbine foliage, so delicate and unobtrusive, but neither blossoms nor buds. After that I keep coming across the small plants, as if my mind has opened up to them. I remember Sharon Butala, in *Wild Stone Heart*, meeting Indian breadroot for the first time after much reading and research. At first sight, she knew it without a doubt.

I make progress by clinging to small islands of bush, and squat to get a closer look at a beautifully clear, bathtub-sized pond, frightening a pinkish frog—I hope it's an at-risk red-legged frog. A short path of stones across a dry creek bed brings me to aromatic heaven: a field of sweet gale! The fragrant leaves are new and soft. I walk among the shrubs with my arms outstretched, making contact, breathing deeply, and see something on the ground—a rusty feather.

On my knees now, I part low branches to find the body of a red-tailed hawk.

It is missing only a few feathers. Did it crash into a tree? Was it attacked by an owl? Hawks are not seen often, like eagles or even ospreys. They are rare, at least to me, especially the red-tailed, whose piercing call is exploited so often by Hollywood, wrongly attributed to eagles most of the time. The sound brings images of an arrow being loosed at a great height, then falling to earth. Red-tailed hawks hunt from a high altitude, plummeting to their prey.

A young Tla-o-qui-aht woman I know makes jewellery from feathers. I want to take her some of the hawk's, but I'm conscious that it is not mine, not some resource from which I presume to help myself. I am not Native, so there might be laws against such an exercise. And part of me wants to leave it in peace.

Suddenly tired and hungry, I take a seat on the end of a log that lies with dozens of others across a lagoon. In the distance I can see the beginning of the lake. I remove a snack from my fanny pack and wonder vaguely about my original fear of this place.

Furtive movement in the corner of my eye, and my body freezes. A henna-brown creature lopes quickly across a log to vanish into the gale. "Mink," I breathe, and yet ... large body, prominent ears ... "No. Marten." Only the second time I've glimpsed one in fourteen years of living in Clayoquot Sound.

A mosquito whines in one ear while a blackfly buzzes fitfully beside the other, entangled in my hair. Wildlife sightings, perhaps ironically, always feel otherworldly to me. Like the glimpsed opening of another dimension. This sighting, surely, was a reward for shifting out of my comfort zone. Human arrogance again? Making it personal, making it *mine*. A sign. But the marten, the hawk and the wildflowers have nothing as well as everything to do with me.

It's getting late, time to think about returning to my regular plane of existence. It won't take as long going back, as I'll hasten my pace, still feeling unseen eyes. My kayak will be bumping up against the forest, high tide snaking the patient rope. The sunset will charge everything aglow. Even the tree trunks at the creek mouth will blush peach-grey like the salmon that feed them. I'll glance at my hands on the paddle and see that my very skin belongs to the sky.

⌒

Three weeks later, after confirming with young Gisele Martin, daughter of Joe (who helped build my greenhouse float), that she's interested in the feathers, I'm back. The bog laurel is almost finished flowering, but the butterwort still purples the ground and white Labrador tea blooms festoon the scrub. I suck from sweet salal flowers and tinier, more almondy evergreen huckleberry flowers. Salmonberries, a fruit coveted by both bears and humans, are beginning to form. And everywhere, new, fresh, *big* bear tracks. Shredded, scattered remains of uprooted skunk cabbages speak of hunger, strength and power.

I clap loudly as I tramp along. "I'M JUST PASSING THROUGH." My voice jars the quiet. Where the forest gives way to the bog meadow, a tree has been vigorously slashed higher than my head; two sliced sections of bark as long as my arm lie on the ground. "I GET THE MESSAGE, I'M JUST PASSING THROUGH."

I'm distracted and heartened by bright sparks of orange-red and yellow dotting the meadow: columbines. I run to each one in turn— taking care where I tread.

Finally, among the sweet gale, the hawk is all feathers and bones. The tail pulls easily from the body; the skull topples off of its own accord. The hawk's talons, however, are closed—locked. They won't budge. There's that power again. Awkwardly, I announce to the surroundings that I am doing this for a Tla-o-qui-aht, a person of this place. I fold hawk body parts into a plastic bag, leaving behind most of the bird's remains. Silently thank the land.

The grouse drums me out as evening falls.

Gisele surprises me with a gift. Ribbon-strands of cedar hang from a bull kelp whipcord encircling a hemp-rope web. The focal piece, tied to an amber bead, is the hawk's big tail feather. Before deciding where to hang the dreamcatcher, I hold it up to the floathouse window to better admire it in natural light. Through it, there is dark movement. My eyes adjust past the central web, focus on the nearest shore.

A bear and her yearling cub are turning over rocks and chewing long strands of shore grass that hang from their mouths like green linguini. The cub lifts a green moss pad from a boulder for the juicy insects underneath and some of the moss breaks off, tumbling into the water with a splash. The cub whirls around and stares. Its mother doesn't even look. She is standing on her hind legs, reaching for ever-higher salal flowers. White yarrow blooms close by, in bright contrast to the animals' luxurious black fur.

Born Out Of This

In elementary school I was usually one of the last chosen for dodge ball teams. This was just one of many reasons I dreaded P.E. class and preferred spending hours in the branches of trees with a book.

My father liked to take my sister and me canoeing. It was the only time his face lost its angry purple blotches.

In high school, my grade eleven P.E. class took a trip to Pitt Meadows outside of Vancouver. Moments after I got into a canoe with my best friend, Maria, it became clear that we were navigationally challenged. We dropped far behind the rest of the class and went in circles or zigzagged, laughing fit to burst or bickering in frustration in turn. As embarrassed and fed up as we were, the river inspired and delighted us, even in the pouring rain.

Soon after moving to Tofino, I noticed a sign for canoe rentals. The water called to me: the secret coves, the bird-rich mud flats and densely forested islands held out on the smooth open hands of low tide. Not being able to steer, I didn't phone. But one of the activists on the blockades was a kayak guide. She taught introductory paddling courses. The boats were narrow, the paddles double bladed. This looked like something I could handle! I decided kayaking might provide me with the new luxury of venturing solo into nature, like riding off into the sunset on a steed that needs no fuel save my own breath.

The November day of the introductory paddling course dawned grey and drizzly. Once I was on the water, legs successfully unfolded inside my kayak, I sealed my sprayskirt around the cockpit rim, sensing the craft as an extension of my body rather than some unruly bathtub. But the harbour threw whitecaps at the class. I soon lagged behind the other students, and required special attention from the instructor. (Flashbacks to a P.E. teacher gripping my hands on a baseball bat, trying to force me to swing with grace and precision before an impatient crowd.)

The last item of the day was self-rescue. It took me half an hour just to get into the wetsuit. My boyfriend and I watched the others take turns tipping upside down in the frigid water, pumping out their boats and hoisting themselves back into their cockpits.

I opted for instructor-rescue.

At least I would get a "taste" of the ocean, said the teacher reassuringly. It was easy to tip, and painless to pull off my sprayskirt, bob up to the surface in my life jacket. But the shock of cold stopped my breath. I could neither gasp nor holler.

My boyfriend was even more of a wimp than I was. He opted out of this exercise entirely, much to my mortification. He watched from shore, calling encouragement as the instructor helped me back into my boat. Each of his utterances only drew attention to his choice to stay dry and not learn. Pursing my salty lips, I wished he would just shut up.

In spite of all that, the course built new confidence, and for the next five years I kayaked around the forty-acre island where we lived, exploring to my heart's content. As I propelled my craft toward home at sunset, the sky erupted volcano-red. I was often followed by harbour seals. Rarely, porpoises surfaced several metres off my bow. If I paddled on a moonless night, the bioluminescence trailed after my paddle tips and stern, a gossamer wake. If I paddled under a full moon, all life seemed pulled to its uncanny face.

The first time I undertake the two-hour paddle from the floathouse to town, I face a strong tide and realize I must have read the tide table dyslexically. Another day, the end of the trip is complicated by vicious white waves, and when I finally reach town, I roll onto the dock to kiss the rope-worn wood, trembling from exertion and the aftershock of terror, my mouth dry from unbroken prayer. If I had tipped, I would have been done for. I still haven't mastered self-rescue.

Commuting to town on better days, I recall a previous life with my British punk boyfriend. He played bass in a band and wrote a song with the chorus line "Commuter zone, leave me alone." He would scream the lyrics about hundreds of office "plods" taking the train sixty miles to London and back every day for their pen-pushing jobs. When I go to work, it's along Lemmens Inlet, and whether it's calm or choppy it's always gorgeous. Commuter zone is smug zone.

There is another large island nearby named Vargas, and one September I sign up for a guided weekend trip around it. The weather looks dodgy; I must be a glutton for punishment. But I have a hankering to meet new people who appreciate the outdoors. The plan is to travel along the outside to Ahous Bay and set up camp. The *outside* ... that means open ocean, where there's nothing between Vargas and Japan but *us*.

The boats are loaded down with gear and we set off. Within minutes, I am falling behind the group of mostly grey-haired enthusiasts. Turns out my five years of experience has been spent doing the "lazy arm": keeping my elbows bent with every stroke instead of stretching them and achieving better momentum.

As we begin to hit big swell at the island's southwest corner, fear seizes me and nausea creeps in. For several tense moments, the two guides whisper together. My lips must be moving because a woman in a double kayak calls over the tumult: "To whom do you pray?"

"I don't know," I yell back, close to panic. "Neptune? Poseidon?"

"Try Venus!" advises her partner from their rear cockpit. Gesturing calmly at the monstrous waves we're riding, she adds, "She was born out of this."

The guides decide to turn back; we'll stay at the Vargas Island Inn. It turns out the women in the double are as relieved as I am. By the time we leave the swell behind, I feel like crawling into a dry, dark cave somewhere. I never did pray to the goddess of love. Is there a goddess of fear? Of seasickness?

Later, mostly recovered thanks to the land under my feet, I join half the group to explore the inside shore while the other half returns to the hell-swells, including a white-bearded man and his wife. The couple has been running a kayak business for a decade, which explains both their fearlessness and their skill.

The next day dawns wet. After a challenging, muddy hike across the island, we all have a sauna. The crab eaten around the table that evening was caught right outside in the bay.

The double-kayak pair, Gretchen and Jo, have a wallpapering business called the Paper Dolls. They tell me that they once papered walls for a "Celtic priestess-poet with scary-looking altars everywhere." Inevitably we find ourselves talking about paranormal phenomena.

I chuckle about my late great-uncle writing a book called *Science of a Witch's Brew*—pyramids, phantom limbs, dowsing with witching wires he shaped from clothes hangers.

Abruptly, the white-bearded man demands: "So what made *you* the skeptic?" He and his wife used to work with a founder of Findhorn, the magical garden in Scotland created from barren ground with the help of fairies and plant devas. I have no answer for him, and silently I wonder what Uncle Bill thought of books like *The Secret Life of Plants*. I don't tell them that the wire Uncle Bill handed me pointed to my birthplace when I held it, or that my niece, Sarah, is a ghost hunter with a paranormal society. In some respects, I'm no skeptic.

The next day fog plugs the entire sound. I decide to stay behind, reminding myself uncomfortably of that moment years ago when my boyfriend chose security over fear and cold water. How judgmental I was! After all, I had also chosen a route easier than self-rescue, and now I'm opting out of hell. Who do I think I am?

I hike and read while the group kayaks the outside. It's all right, damn it, to be an inside-paddler. It's quiet, peaceful, serene, even healing if you can avoid the more macho whale-watching zodiac drivers. Later, I paddle past calm, safe, empty beaches, and the next day as we journey back to town there is no sign of my "lazy arm."

Often when I tell people about my lifestyle they can't believe someone so susceptible to seasickness enjoys paddling and floathouse living. They have a point. After various traumatic experiences on the ocean, why do I always live by it? Or *on* it, for that matter? My Celtic ancestors paddled in currachs, made by stretching up to three animal hides over a wooden frame and stitching them together with leather thongs. (Currachs are still used in western Ireland today and have changed little in design.) The Celts also used dugout canoes, carved from the split trunk of an oak tree and propelled with broad-bladed wooden paddles. I never confessed my heritage to Gretchen and Jo.

If they knew, would they be afraid to come paper my walls? Or, do they now have their own altars dedicated to the birthplace of Venus?

Paddling is in my blood (even if I can't steer a currach or a dugout). It's part of my heritage—not an uncommon legacy. That means that the ocean itself is part of me. I ride it on my commute home, avoiding windy weather, seeking the pleasing sight of cormorants on rocks, spreading their wings to dry. Timeless simplicity, unsullied seascape: this is my home, Venus protect it.

This far up the inlet one's work schedule does not always match the tide's, and eventually I am diagnosed with frozen shoulders. Self-rescue comes in the form of a four-stroke outboard.

A framed photo card of a harbour seal, in gold matting, sits on my desk. The animal is underwater, near the surface. It gazes directly into the camera, flanked by green-gold bull kelp, one fin partially wrapped in the caressing seaweed. The seal has long whiskers as white as waves. A moment of connection, without fear.

Somewhere in Clayoquot Sound, ancient trees are falling and a girl is skipping P.E. class to seek the wild. She might be reading in a tree, joining her parents on a blockade, paddling as hard as she can, or drifting with the current. One thing is certain: she knows self-rescue.

AVIAN FREE-FOR-ALL

It's our town's umpteenth annual Pacific Rim Shorebird Festival. At the slideshow, after half an hour of trying to follow the presenter's pointers for identifying individual species within huge, diverse flocks of birds, my friend Maryjka blurts out miserably from the front row: "They're all damn brown."

I laugh with the others. Even the birding expert smiles sympathetically. But Maryjka is a glutton for punishment; she goes birding every Sunday morning with the local guide, other residents and tourists.

Part of me dreads this time of year because of people who let their dogs run freely on the beaches. Inevitably, dogs chase shorebirds, who desperately need to rest and find food before they resume their migratory odyssey of thousands of kilometres. One day if you visit, you might be handed a pamphlet or fridge magnet that says,

"Give Shorebirds Space on the Beach!" Clayoquot Sound is an oasis for all kinds of wildlife because it contains most of the island's last few pristine watersheds. The sound is a crucial feeding ground to migratory shorebirds—they make it a stopover on their biannual journeys up and down the coast because of a certain avian free-for-all called the mudflats.

Rumours of peregrine falcons severing ducks' heads from their bodies catch my interest, so I tag along with the birders one clear, cool spring morning. Maryjka drives, and the small assembly carpools from the meeting point to the mudflat shore on the calm side of the peninsula.

When the receding tide reveals the flats, by late April flocks of up to twenty thousand shorebirds may be seen pulling small prey from the mud. These birds usually travel here by night since during the day falcons and merlins prey on them.

So when do they get to rest? I wonder.

As the organizers set up five spotting scopes, I gaze at Lone Cone. It's framed by the limbs of a gnarled alder standing over the wet, flattened shore grass. The ebbing ocean is smooth, mirroring the sky. Distant glaciers provide contrast to clumps of forested islands in our immediate vicinity. A rooster crows from the Botanical Gardens across a small bay, and a mallard guffaws somewhere closer. I wait for someone to lower one of the scopes to my meagre height of five foot two.

We are all locals on this day; everyone knows one another. Barb, the naturalist, is already counting birds and making notes. I didn't know this was a counting expedition. I haven't even looked through a scope yet and am suddenly feeling rebelliously lazy.

"Actually I'm hoping to see wolves as well," Maryjka announces.

"Oh, we're serious birders. We ignore wolves if we see them," quips Darlene.

Kathleen is exalting over the black-bellied plovers. "Aren't they gorgeous? For some reason they remind me of skunks."

I step up and peer through the scope short enough for me. On shore, a couple of female mallards doze in a patch of bladderwrack sea-weed—a quintessential west coast scene. I find the plovers. They have black chests and bellies and are with hundreds of other birds. I listen to the talk around me, so I know we are watching dunlins, sander-lings, widgeons, sandpipers, pintails, shovelers, mergansers, and one green-winged teal.

Maryjka materializes at my elbow. "How are you doing?"

In a mutter only she can hear, I answer, "Ducks, dunlins, dowitch-ers. They're all damn brown."

She throws back her head and laughs like a mallard. "I suggest you look again at the dowitchers."

Good call. There are only eleven of them, heads and shoulders above everybody else: tall and impressive, dark and handsome, with beautiful long bills.

"How is it that so many of these birds' names sound poetic?" I murmur. "Sanderling ... sandpiper ... dunlin ... plover."

"Yeah. Not 'gadwall' though," she snickers.

I adjust the scope. "What was that?" she says sharply.

"It was the scope squeaking."

"Oh." My friend looks slightly crestfallen.

I hear male rufous hummingbirds zipping from flower to flower in the salmonberry bushes behind us, and Maryjka says she can't hear them. A winter wren is singing its heart out a little farther away. Dar-lene can't hear that. Suddenly I am struck by the prospect of my own hearing diminishing as I age. I religiously wear earplugs to every punk rock show, but still ...

How I feel for my older friends this morning. Standing here, I take the horror further in my mind, imagining a silent world, bereft of birdsong, of birds' calls, of the air sifting their feathers as they fly. How should I ever know the presence of nighthawks if I were no longer stopped in my tracks by the *boom* of their wings?

"Are you going to use that scope, or daydream?" Maryjka asks. She is almost as short as I am. I let her have it and walk away toward the tote of cookies and hot chocolate. The guide, Adrian Dorst, is saying, "I was with Robert Bateman in 1960 when I saw my first dunlin at Turkey Point, Lake Erie."

Kathleen returns him to the present by asking him to identify a small group of birds.

"Greater yellowlegs," he replies, adding, "That's funny, because they're behaving more like lesser yellowlegs."

Marvelling at Adrian's deep knowledge of birds and their subtle behavioural differences, I munch on a cookie and continue thumbing through a bird book, wondering what he means but not asking. I am, in fact, intimidated. Looking at the pictures in the guidebook, I note that red-breasted mergansers have punk hairstyles. Crests, I should say. Do they ever feel crestfallen?

Someone calls out, "Fifty mallards." I return to the scope and jostle Maryjka for it. The shorebirds—perhaps thousands now—are feeding in shallow water barely covering the mud, bobbing like high-powered machines as a pair of ravens cry their stone-down-the-well calls far away. A pair of magnificent male mallards cruises in the midst of this feeding frenzy, dwarfing the birds surrounding them.

Adrian reckons there are seven hundred dunlins! And six bald eagles, plus the odd kingfisher and great blue heron. With thirty-nine obliging buffleheads.

"What's this little thing flying up?" I ask him.

"Merlin!" he says almost instantly. Everyone looks up. The bird lands at the very top of a hemlock tree and poses, supremely aloof. Every scope swings on its tripod. Such a little thing! Fluffy, with a tiny exquisite death-hook of a beak. The narrow feathers above the eyes are lighter than the rest of the face, giving the appearance of eyebrows. It hangs around for ten minutes, then takes off.

That's when we notice the flock of shorebirds wheeling around in the distance, appearing and disappearing like cloud puffs, in and out of some private vortex, riding the cracks between dimensions. Surely they are doing it for sheer pleasure, yet what of the energy it takes? Adrian brings me back to reality by blaming the merlin's visit.

Even without falcons and severed heads, I am satisfied with the outing. When a couple of large unleashed dogs meander through our group, their owner whistling from the other end of the shore, I am gratified to sense our collective disapproval. And when we notice several large, ungainly shapes on the opposite mudflats that turn out to be seven pubescent boys rather than wolves, I chuckle at the folly of youth: barefoot on cold, sucking mud for something to do. A fascinating species.

And I get a kick out of the birding lexicon.

"I see a black butt! He's tipping, showing it off."

"You mean the guy on the right, next to the widgeon?"

To top off our morning, we spot someone waving at us from the Botanical Gardens. It's Ornery Ralph and Tsunami Dave (many people here have mysterious nicknames, which nevertheless aid in identification). Ralph has his own scope and is watching birds (and us). Dave is doing tai chi, or weights; we can't be certain which.

When the birding expedition is over, I go home to my little houseboat where hummers are fighting over the feeder I have put up, the resident loons are calling to each other and four common mergansers are tugging morsels off my land lines. A lonely feather floats away from me on the current. I hope the shorebirds will get some sleep.

MONKEY MARTEN

On an overcast May day, while my friend Corinne is visiting, a river otter lunches under the deck beneath her feet, a mink scampers up and down the rocks on shore and a merganser climbs on the dock. Most days are much quieter here, without human conversation, with little spectacular wildlife action that I'm aware of. But Corinne departs impressed.

One spring I keep finding tiny droppings on the narrowest deck. Someone says I must have a mouse. But why would a mouse swim all the way over? Could it smell my compost all the way from shore, and be that hungry? Where could it be hiding on board? The theory doesn't fit.

That same season a bat flits by every dusk and circles the float just once before vanishing to hunt. Almost as though it has emerged *from* the float. I study the wall directly over the tiny droppings; there's a crack in the wood. During the day I hear batty squeaking coming from the area. I worry a little about damage to the wall of my home, but mostly this new situation seems so very *cool.* Thrilling, even: I live with *Myotis lucifugus.*

So many miracles over the years. The times merganser mums have toodled along with their trains of seven ducklings. The time a "snowberry clearwing," or hummingbird moth, uncurls its proboscis at the hanging flowers. The times of wolves. The less pleasant occasion an eagle terrorizes a pair of buffleheads.

But the marten is different. It has something the others do not. It appears to be motivated by curiosity.

In a poem, I write:

bold curious marten
> of rich fur and semi-retractable claws
> scaling the walls
>> peering down from the roof
> scuttling through garden beds
>> hearing me speak softly to you
>>> sniffing me without fear
dangling by your rear toes from my boat
> dog-paddling back to shore
>> I will say your name[37]

At low tide one overcast day (there are a lot of those kinds of days) something light brown moves on the creekside deck. I stand up, but it's fast. I hear the sound of clawed feet climbing up the northeast wall and then scampering across the roof. Quietly I let myself out onto the

37   Christine Lowther, "Say the Names," in *My Nature.*

greenhouse deck and look up. A marten comes to the edge of the roof and looks down.

Like the one I glimpsed between the sweet gale field and the lake, this animal is a light henna with delicate ears and a pointed face. Its body is long and lean, its rich, full tail a shade darker than the rest. It looks down at me, full in my face, and doesn't even blink. Instead, it scales the wall, head first, with powerful claws. I'm not afraid either; it's making its way toward me, yes, but it's interested in everything—the wall, the clothesline, the heavy hook for hanging baskets or windchimes. When it reaches the floor it barely notices the gap between floathouse deck and greenhouse deck. It just keeps sniffing and peering at planters and solar panels before moving right past boring old me into the greenhouse. It gives the compost bucket a passing sniff up on hind legs, then leaps into the garden bed. It's too early in the season for much to be growing yet, but still, I make a point of walking in a few steps and saying, "Hey, c'mon now."

Out it goes, bypassing me again, and I follow. It turns and sniffs my feet as I stand still. Then it scarpers down the west dock and stares longingly to shore. So different from a mink, who is not inquisitive but fierce, and at home in the water (its body streamlined as it swims). The marten, an arboreal mammal, comes back and climbs into my boat, up onto its port side, still staring at the forest. Low tide will bring shore a lot closer; still, another swim is required for it to get back to dry land. And so it lowers itself until it is hanging by its rear toe-claws from my boat! Then it dog-paddles back to shore, keeping its head above water.

I find faint marks on my boat's lip, and footprints creekside where it first came on board. I know that if I had opened the door, it would have scuttled inside my house. That curious.

LOVING EIK

*The tree which moves some to tears of joy is in the eyes of others
only a green thing that stands in the way.*

—William Blake,
The Letters of William Blake Together with His Life

*For the Karen in the forests of northern Thailand, the umbilical
cord of a baby would be tied to a tree; the spirit of the child dwelt
there, and to harm the tree would be to harm the child; the ritual
thus intricately linked person to tree.*

—Jay Griffiths, *Wild: An Elemental Journey*

At the last judgement we shall all be trees.

—Margaret Atwood, *The Journals of Susanna Moodie*

TREE WAS A SEEDLING WHEN GENGHIS KHAN BUILT HIS EMPIRE

HOW THE EIK STREET TREE IS DIVIDING TOFINO

KILL IT BEFORE IT HURTS SOMEBODY

GIRDLES AND GUYS WILL KEEP TOFINO'S HUGE CEDAR ALIVE

IT JUST NEEDS PRUNING
                    —headlines from various newspapers at the time

It might not be an overstatement to say that Emily Carr was obsessed with western red cedars. She painted hundreds. Some of these paintings were *Red Cedar* (1933), *Scorned as Timber, Beloved of the Sky* (1935), *Laughing Forest* (c. 1939) and *Cedar Sanctuary* (c. 1942). The Eik (pronounced "Ike") Street tree is a red cedar in Tofino, the town that was headquarters for logging blockades that changed the course of Canadian history in the early 1990s. "Trees are the culture of this land," once commented a Tofino resident. Perhaps it is that simple, yet old trees are something more. Ancient trees like eight-hundred-year-old Eik have so many dimensions: as symbols of the wild and continuity, as elders from the past, as living records of history and as ecosystems within themselves.

Many like Eik are also honkin' huge, their massive trunks streaming with ribbons of cedar bark, their evergreen boughs swaying gracefully overhead. For west coast First Nations, the bark still makes clothing, blankets, baskets, masks and more. Giant trees just across the harbour from Eik on Meares Island's Big Trees Trail are also red cedars. Tourists pay to visit them. In 2001 when Eik started featuring in the news, visitors began coming to Tofino specifically to see this one tree on a corner of district land beside the highway approaching downtown.

Don Bottrell, an award-winning arborist hired by people who love Eik, said: "It is uncommon to see a first-growth tree in an urban setting; this is the only one in Canada, if not the entire Pacific Northwest."[38]

There used to be another across the road from Eik, a thousand-year-old red cedar called the Millennium Tree, but it was cut down to make way for development in the fall of 1999. Many local children and residents grieved its loss. The two together were a gateway to Clayoquot Sound, UN-designated biosphere reserve.

Because the Eik tree is hollow inside, Tofino Council and district staff could be held liable if Eik's forty-nine metres were to fall and hurt someone at the development slated to begin next to it. Two council-hired arborists (one of them known as "the Executioner" among some of his own colleagues) deemed the tree hazardous. And so began a complicated, empassioned struggle around the tree. Council condemned it at first. Before I got involved, local residents tied an honourary medal around the trunk and, later, a SAVE ME banner. Local author and artist Michael Curnes organized our town's first official community portrait, and hundreds of us—schoolchildren and adults—posed under Eik. All of these events took place, I might add, in relentless pouring rain.

Council vetoed the pending development to allow for further assessment of the tree. Eventually, though, after we had exhausted all the usual legal avenues—a petition, letters to council and the local paper, publicity stunts, meetings—a morning arrived with tree removers and their equipment. Full of dread, I didn't think I'd leave my cabin, but I thought about what Michael had said at one of our meetings: "It doesn't leave a lot of hope for the thousands of other eight-hundred-year-old trees still standing in Clayoquot Sound if we can't save this one tree right here among us." Moreover, I loved this particular tree.

38   Appeared in the *Gulf Island Gazette*.

Sounds dramatic, maybe, but love propelled me out the door. Trying to feel calm, hoping somehow to go unnoticed, I walked past the crowd, the media and the police, toward the fallers and their enormous chainsaw.

A police officer called after me, requesting I leave the danger zone. I knew and liked him, so I turned around but kept walking backwards, shrugging apologetically. "Sorry, but you'll have to arrest me."

He smiled kindly. "I'd rather not have to do that." And he didn't, because it turned out that he couldn't make any arrests without an injunction that council would have to apply for, against their own electorate. (They did apply, later.)

Over the ensuing hours, various police officers, the three friendly fallers and the head of Public Works tried coaxing me to leave the fall zone, but by now I wasn't the only one inside it. Three other women had joined me. After a couple of hours the authorities gave up, the fallers went back to Port Alberni and I stayed at the tree all day, taking media calls. Supporters brought me food. Then two young men approached and said they were willing to scale the tree and occupy it.

"Do you have any experience?" I asked.

"Rock-climbing."

I told them about my friend Kathy, who had fallen from a tree in the Walbran Valley, breaking her back. She spent nine months in hospital. But they weren't fazed. Young and enthusiastic, they had neither training nor gear. Late that night, with the help of two forest canopy–platform experts who had travelled from Victoria, Brad Lindey and Dominic Beaulieu climbed twenty-six metres up the tree. Once they reached the big branches, they set up hammocks and tarps. I could go home now.

The feeling going around was that council was our only hope: they had the power—the tree "belonged" to the district. But they refused to meet with us until the developer with plans for the land next to Eik called a meeting of all interested parties. This was different. I was used to being a sort of fringe shit disturber and here I was, along with many others from our new group, the Tofino Natural Heritage Society (TNHS), meeting with a developer and local government (the same government that was suing me for interfering with their plans for the tree).

The meeting began with Don Bottrell, the arborist we'd hired, explaining that Eik was "dynamic" and that risks could be mitigated if it was supported with some kind of buttress. Don and his team had spent hours and hours on site, doing every kind of test imaginable, even returning late at night during a howling storm to measure the tree's movement and examining each and every branch to make sure it was safe. He agreed with the other arborists that removing the dead crown would relieve some of the perceived hazard. Don offered to top Eik for free, a complicated job and thus a great act of generosity.

After some discussion amongst all the parties, the developer pledged to find the money to build a bracing structure for Eik. He also promised to help come up with funds for the structure itself, which could reach one hundred thousand dollars. As the meeting ended, a friend tearfully said to me, "This tree wants to live."

This was a good ending, but with a catch. The developer wanted to build more tourist condos than he had originally planned. These would be on mudflat waterfront where locals had lived in a few modest houses for decades, land that's part of a First Nations midden where Native people historically dug for clams in the mud. There also used to be skulls in sea caves there until a German man was charged with grave pillaging. Stories within stories. Next, George Patterson, owner of Tofino Botanical Gardens, put forward a proposal to transplant Eik. "I've moved big trees before," he said. I could never tell if he was joking or not.

As the tale turned around and around, I found myself busier than ever, my life taken over by a new career: saving Eik. Sometimes this meant delivering Chinese takeout to the tree sitters; other times it meant dealing with their urine jugs and crap bucket, or getting lectured by the RCMP sergeant. Dom and Brad promised the police they weren't using drugs, enticing young female passersby, or hootin' and hollerin' all night. Every weekend at 1:00 a.m. the bars would close, and someone would slingshot rocks up into the tree. Or fireworks. And once, a man revved his chainsaw at Eik's base, threatening the guys' lives.

I learned some of Eik's settler history from a neighbour. Lumber for houses was brought here by boat, and Eik was used to pulley the wood up to the land where the homes were built. Years later Eik was used for another purpose: locals would drop off their expired cars and the neighbour would crush them against the tree with his bulldozer.

One day CHEK TV asked their local cameraman to go up the tree and interview its inhabitants. Next thing I heard, the developer's lawyer went up. Then a friend of Dominic's. Then a local photographer whose pictures appeared on the front pages of newspapers. Meanwhile, I was having recurring nightmares about heights.

"Hey Chris!" called Dom from on high. "You're next!"

At the bottom of Eik, the harness reminded me of 1970s London punk fashion. The climbing rope was the width of a dime: not reassuring. "There's no danger involved," Brad told me.

You're seventeen, I thought. *You're probably not in touch with your mortality.*

I knew it would be hard work. I remembered something written by Julia Butterfly Hill, a woman who lived in a threatened California redwood tree for two years: "Loosen, move up, stand, loosen, move up, lean back, loosen, move up, stand, loosen, move up, lean back."[39] To me it was more like: pull legs up with sore stomach muscles, push tired arm up, thrust hips forward, stand, grunt. I could only do three cycles at a time, then rest. Voices on the ground faded, the traffic grew louder, the industrial noise across the road at the new quarry mess assaulted me, and the breeze blew Eik's green boughs around me.

By the time I reached the first big branch twenty-six metres up, I was utterly spent. It took Brad five minutes to get there. It had taken me twenty-five. I wouldn't look anywhere but at the bark before my face, in case the faraway ground met my eyes. I was panting and shaking. Yet Dom wanted me to stand on this branch so he could switch the ropes on my harness. I wouldn't move. Eventually he grabbed my harness and hauled me onto the first net, their "balcony." It was some kind of old fish net, flimsy looking, held to Eik by mere strings. Meanwhile he—in Gore-Tex jacket, fleece pants and bare feet—was dancing around from branch to branch like a monkey. I didn't stay long. I was so looking forward to being grounded again that the moment of going over the edge was welcome. Then, wheeee! all the way down.

Concerned locals packed the next council meeting, where a motion to grant a forty-five-day reprieve was passed and negotiations began. Dominic and Brad descended to the ground amid cheers, applause and hugs.

Michael soon orchestrated an art auction to help raise funds to pay for the "groundbreaking, world-class project" that was to be the support structure. Thirty artists, including Mark Hobson, Robert Bateman, Annie George, Briony Penn and Daniel Izzard, contributed their work and we made twenty thousand dollars. It was deeply moving to see the many beautiful paintings of Eik. But the design proposed

39   Julia Butterfly Hill, *The Legacy of Luna: The Story of a Tree, a Woman and the Struggle to Save the Redwoods* (Scarborough, ON: HarperOne, 2001).

by the developer's engineer was vetoed by council, and the developer withdrew his support. Now we were on our own.

Next, structural engineer David Romain came up with the idea of a steel girdle plus guy wires that, over time, would weather to blend with the trunk's colour. The wires would be set slightly to slack, allowing for sway and growth. The girdle would not prevent tree failure, but could contain it. The girdle collars could be loosened over the years, maintaining the dignity and natural expansion of Eik. There would be regular inspections. This design proposal was accepted; work began.

For our ceremony at the project's end, we were honoured that Tla-o-qui-aht elder Levi Martin sang a prayer. Letters of support from the prime minister, the premier, the minister of natural heritage and the minister of environment were read to the crowd. It was a beautiful, clear sunny day. I didn't care a fig that some cartoonists made fun of our support structure. I may even have chuckled.

From the folks who brought you COMMUNITY HALL CHAINSAW MASSACRE and BIOSPHERE BLOODBATH …
NIGHT OF THE LIVING DEADFALL
They chained it down…
They made it live…
They turned it into a freak…
Now it wants revenge!
THE TERROR NEVER ENDS!

➤

Sticker: FREE the TREE! *TOFINO, BC.*

"It's outrageous to spend a hundred thousand dollars on one tree," someone said to me soon after. "I mean, that's my mortgage."

I thought of the sacrifice made by our heroes Brad and Dom, and smiled. It's a tree's life. And it might feel like it sometimes, but a mortgage doesn't take eight hundred years to pay off. Without using taxpayers' money, a creative solution was found. In 2011, eagles built a nest in Eik's high branches.

In Europe, 500-year-old trees are revered; even 250-year-old trees are held in awe and fought for. In England, where I lived for five years, only yew trees commonly live longer, and they are considered sacred, often enclosed in churchyards where the church had deliberately been built next to the tree hundreds of years previously. Of course I wish Eik could have been allowed to live without armour, and yes, it can seem crazy that we had to go to such lengths to save one tree in a bio-sphere reserve, here, where 932 people were arrested defending the rainforest in one summer back in '93. On the other hand, the fact that we care about ancient trees is clearly visible here, and I think Emily Carr would appreciate our efforts. Our choice was to support it or stump it. I've heard of a five-hundred-thousand-dollar bracing struc-ture for a tree in the US. I have seen several structurally supported trees in England. I have seen every branch of an oak lovingly propped from the ground up, its trunk buoyed in belts like Eik's.

"A tree of such age and majesty is priceless," said my friend Maryj-ka Mychajlowycz, a TNHS director, at the close of 2001. "You can't replace it. People commission totem poles and sculpture for ten thou-sand dollars or more. And here we have a monument that is both liv-ing art and living history ... I fell in love with this tree. It was within minutes of being cut. And now it's lived to see another year—perhaps hundreds more."

Pieces Of A Floater's Life

QUEEN OF THE DEAD

I was on a second date with a man when he suddenly said, "You know what you are? A trauma queen."

This after listening for an hour to his life story full of tragedy and hardship. Was I wrong to figure on contributing some of my own? Not to compare, but to share: to draw us closer, fellow survivors, friends. Aren't dates supposed to be engaged in a dialogue, a dance for two?

The straightforwardness of floathouse time (my real gauge for quality time) can be a balm for such mortifications. The wildlife's indifference to me somehow does not wound. I can shake my baffled head at the complexity of pain we humans live with and spread around, and watch the water dance, washing all away for a while. Maybe retreating here is hiding. Maybe it is being free to express emotion. Trauma queen? This place can take all the royal rage I need to expel.

I was here when I received the radio-phone call to tell me of my grandmother's death. Whenever someone I love dies, I go into nature and speak their name: an anguished wail, an urgent whisper, a barked command or a farewell caress: Ramon, Ben, Damon, Paulette, Freya, Gael, Niky.

After the call about my grandmother, I stood on deck and called out her name to the mountain. Virginia: Gram.

DREAMING DISASTER

In the wake of the southeast Asian tsunami on Boxing Day 2004, I experience strange dreams. I am in Vancouver when the wave comes, with my ten-year-old nephew Rowan. The destruction reaches our toes, then recedes. We are untouched; we are not even shocked.

This dream is followed by another: orcas surround my float. Several pods congregating with their young, facing the shore in a peak high tide. They are here for some ancient, unexplainable reason, and they're not doing much of anything: surfacing to breathe, submerging again. They face the land, as if waiting for some signal. Rod Palm appears, Clayoquot Sound's orca expert, observing from his boat. The presence of these whales is a miracle. Later, my floathouse sinks for no apparent reason.

When I write down the dream many weeks later I recognize the behaviour of spawning salmon in the whales' odd conduct. In real life, the chum salmon come into bays containing streams where they were born—not mine, its conditions aren't quite perfect. They face the shore, waiting, floating, conserving energy for the water to be deep enough for them to swim in and use the gravel beds to bury their eggs.

In a few days, in waking life, my aluminum boat sinks in heavy winter rains due to a faulty bilge pump. The motor requires hundreds of dollars' worth of repair.

Due to the town's exquisitely vulnerable location, two tsunami warning sirens were finally installed at North Chesterman Beach and Cox Bay in 2011. Not a dream.

STOWAWAY

The silence runs deep; loneliness lurks as evening falls, soup simmers on the woodstove, and I peruse my books. Next morning dawns so sunny that I don't bother with a fire, even though the hot tub is frozen solid. (Its use is limited to the summer months.) The daffodils in the greenhouse have burst their sheaths. How many more days? I long for bees.

Garbage in the water is a human's responsibility, even a small piece of styrofoam, so I get into the kayak and paddle toward a chunk that has appeared from nowhere. Approach reveals a stowaway. The biggest wolf spider ever? No. It is a giant cave … field … primitive monster cricket? No, it's too big for any of these. Whatever it is, all that's keeping it from certain death is a little piece of styrofoam.

I will be the hero and save it, placing it carefully on the rocks and taking the foam back to the cabin.

When I prod the insect awake, it leaps in panic as if catapulted, and instead of heading for the forest it lands in the cold water, instantly sinking in a tangle of long legs. Can something go from being that lively to split-second death? I scoop it up and feel it stir against my palm. It fills my whole hand, legs sticking out between my fingers. I place it farther up the rocks nearer the trees. But the same thing happens, so this time I throw the cricket as far as I can into the trees. Damned if the thing doesn't come hurling itself back, and this time I can't find it in the water. I should have beached the kayak and hiked deep into the forest. I take the piece of styrofoam back to the float and drop it in my garbage bag, sadly unheroic.

More Dreaming

I dream of waking up and looking out the window. I see islands far below and realize that my entire establishment has come loose and is flying, whipped up like Dorothy on her way to Oz. Luckily we land safely in the harbour, speeding faster than Zodiacs; all the boats have to move out of the way fast. My partner is being dragged along behind. As he tries to shout out instructions, water fills his mouth and he is pulled under again. I awake truly, laughing and shaking. How many more gales? Some years, the stormiest months have been April and May.

Like Hanging from a Cliff until, Miraculously, a Foothold

After a perfectly hideous day in town trying to be a good salesperson, I look forward to a good cry once I reach the float. On my way to the dock, I walk past a tree full of blossoms, wondering if I will ever feel again the way blossoming trees usually make me feel. The boat ride is moonlit, gorgeous. When I step from my boat onto the deck, the load of despair evaporates as if it never existed.

The moon lights up the cabin, which is warm enough not to start a fire. I am in bed with a hot water bottle before nine o'clock, content. Saved, again.

In the morning the greenhouse offers a container bursting with wide-open daffodils and delicate white crocuses. I have them all before me now in the sunshine, the daffs nodding. Everything but the creek, a gull or two and the dripping of melting frost is quite still. Tide is rising. I want to do as little as possible, no thinking or worrying. Even writing is a distraction from being here, taking this place in as deeply as possible. It is my medicine and all too soon I'll have to leave again.

I try not to think about it. I find it scary when work and endless interactions with people take me to a state of incoherence. I don't turn on the radio when I'm like this because I'll feel nauseous if I hear another word. Gulls' cries, kingfishers' chatterings are fine, even pleasant to my tired ears. But not human language. When I was a teenager, I loved crowds at peace marches and rock concerts. I was in my element. How things change!

The warm stillness wakes a large bumblebee that matches the daffodils: yellow, but with a deep orange centre. She can barely get around, struggling with gravity. I know that a couple of weeks will make the difference: she'll be flying with the precision she lacks now. She clambers with difficulty into the heart of an exquisite crocus. Probing clumsily, she finds her dusty-sweet treasure. Revels and rolls in her fumbling way, mauling the pollen-soaked prize until sated. She turns, blinks through pollen and veers away over the water.

Watching her go, my glance is caught by yet another mystery. Sunlight illuminates a graceful billowing spider thread. It has been cast across the water and let go. Did the spider use it to travel across the vastness of the bay? Is such a thing possible? Later, another gossamer thread blows close to me and I take it between thumb and forefinger. Make it dance some more.

ACQUIRING FURNITURE

I lean against the counter and watch the waders swinging like a body from the drying rack above the woodstove. My eyes fall on the dresser, a pretty light blue with dogwood flowers for handles, a blue that goes perfectly with the ceiling. You'd think the dresser came with the floathouse. But this dresser, this perfectly respectable dresser (missing only one handle), is far more intriguing than that. In fact, it typifies the eccentricity of Clayoquot Sound. I know what you're thinking. The eccentricity of Clayoquot Sound in a dresser?

It happened like this: Warren was on a mission one day out in the sound, zooming happily along, when he saw something blue far away. As his boat came nearer he saw that it was made of straight lines and was something unnatural, something human-made. It seemed to be standing on the ocean. Curiosity hooked, he slowed the motor and approached. It was the dresser. Eel grass and other sea weeds poked out of the open drawers.

Clunk went the bottom of the boat, and he understood. The dresser was resting on a peninsula of rock just under the surface of the rising tide. Warren felt he had no choice but to save a useful piece of furniture before it was claimed forever by the sea.

"It almost seemed a shame to take it," he told me dreamily afterwards. "It made such a surreal scene. Like a Pink Floyd album sleeve."

But what a mystery. Why was the dresser unwanted? Who put it out on the rocks in the middle of the sound? Which eccentric placed it so enticingly? Yet it had seaweed in its drawers. Could it have floated and landed so perfectly right-side-up on the peninsula? Why would someone dump a big blue dresser into the ocean? Conversely, how could such a thing fall in accidentally?

Some weeks later, Maryjka and I were paddling in God's Pocket close to shore, watching eagles fishing. Rounding a bend, Maryjka spotted an old wooden deck chair on the stones. I was dubious of adorning the float with it until we got close up and saw the funky paint job: swirls, the woman symbol, the man symbol, circles and curved lines in bright colours. Perfect. Eccentric.

UNEXPECTED ACTION

> All the diamonds in this world
> that mean anything to me
> are conjured up by wind and sunlight
> sparkling on the sea.
>
> —Bruce Cockburn, "All the Diamonds"[40]

I am mesmerized by water diamonds, chips of sunlight dancing across the breeze-blown surface, sparks of pure delight. They have no purpose other than their feel-good one, at least not that I can see. Their constant movement is somehow comforting.

I fall asleep on the deck watching them, and am awakened by the cooling of my skin and the absence of light when the sun goes behind Lone Cone. I moan in protest: too soon, too soon. It's the hardest part

---

40 Bruce Cockburn, "All the Diamonds," lyrics written by Bruce Cockburn (SOCAN), copyright Rotten Kiddies Music LLC (BMI).

of the day, I think, deciding that if I make an appointment with the chiropractor, it will be at the end of the day so that I'll feel sun on my face in town a while longer before coming back in the dusk.

Following these ruminations, I take the kayak out, chasing sunshine. Once in its glow I turn around to face the floathouse. There is the path of diamonds. I paddle toward it, wondering if it will make like a mirage and never let me catch it. But suddenly I am among them. I am *in* the diamonds.

I wish I had someone to share this moment with. I move closer to the bay's resident gulls, Phoebe and Loopy as I think of them. They are calling to each other in loud mimicry even when they are right next to each other.

A seal surfaces now and again, its breathing sweet to my ears. Fish are jumping, and over by the oyster farm the water churns as if a whole school has been spooked by an eagle flying over. An eagle *has* been making swipes at them, but she's perched in a snag now.

I peer through the binoculars. It is the other seal; its head appears amid the action, one or two fish flopping out just in front of it, trying to get away. Is this a game for the seal, a cornucopious smorgasbord, or is it merely frustrating? Is it like humans at a buffet, not knowing where to look first?

The show moves slowly closer, and my seal and two gulls watch too.

There must be more than one school, or else a single, vast one has been divided. The surface-nipping (insect-nabbing) approaches my position. I have been stone-still for many minutes. Phoebe casually plucks a morsel from the water with her bill: that easy.

It occurs to me to stop looking at the water and gaze into it instead. The timing is perfect. A school of thousands of beautiful white-blue shimmering fish swims haphazardly but in a unit toward me. How do the front ones decide on a direction? Their large eyes, wide open, do not tell.

The long, sinuous line of bodies passes under me and is gone, but I only have to watch the surface to know its progress.

I pick up the binoculars again and search for the second seal. It must have rushed its school, because about two hundred fish leap into the air. My jaw drops. The seal's smooth back curves above the water and disappears. The gulls go over to investigate.

I lower the glasses. My seal cruises nearby, staring nonchalantly at me. Pacific harbour seals can dive to 420 metres and remain submerged as long as twenty-eight minutes. Males have a life span of twenty years, females thirty. I look, perplexed at how to pinpoint age or gender from such a face.

There's still sunshine on the far shore, where a barred owl calls matter-of-factly. From the forest hugging the creek, a ruffed grouse continues to drum.

Now I change my mind. A chiropractic appointment will have to happen early in the day. I wouldn't want to miss this action-packed time. I follow the last few diamonds home.

SPRING EQUINOX

The greenhouse has nurtured multi-headed narcissus to greet me this trip, after another work week in town. I was thorough with my headlamp last night, collecting slugs. Where do they come from? I guess their eggs arrive with the finished compost soil I add to the beds and containers. I used to dispose of them by throwing them overboard. But who needs that kind of karma? Now I put them in a container with some greens, and in the morning I paddle over to shore to deposit them in their native habitat. Some of them are downright beautiful, with geometrically even patterns along their backs. Every one is different. A brown blob, a fat striped green comma, a pale yellow oozer, a tan hyphen with black specks and waving tentacles, a colourless, translucent teardrop. All growing up to be rainforest banana slugs.

It has not been a relaxing day so far. Too much untangling to be done from the last storm, including my water line. No running water. A lot of struggling while trying not to flip over in the kayak. Endeavouring to see the positive: the mint has grown profusely. I look forward to months of fresh tea, filling the kettle with lemon balm leaves, wintermint, chocolate mint, pineapple mint and bee balm.

While writing, I hear a strange new sound from the forest. Like the impossibly sped-up hammering of some woodpecker inside a cave or hollow tree. Too fast. Could it be some gutteral statement from a raven I've somehow never caught? The flowers are wilting in the hot sun, so perhaps it is an exotic species just visiting during the unseasonal warmth.

The sky at night is like a city so full of stars once the first thin crescent moon is gone behind the mountain. Lone Cone is a misnomer. Its swellings and dips undulate gradually down from the sky, as Orion's belt slips one star at a time behind the tree line in two places at once. Air and liquid. A bright star or planet keeps me company for hours of happy sleeplessness until it follows Orion. I blink and it's gone, and then my position or branches shift and it shines out again, but fainter. Or it disappears from the sky but its reflection still glows. When it's finally gone for good the sky seems less interesting; there's nothing as bright. An owl calls from a distance as my eyes close.

Pure beauty wakes me in the morning. I lie here smiling, watching the early sunlight dance on the ceiling. I know there is gardening to do, but I only want to sit on deck and listen to the creek and its underlying silence. To spend time just being here.

RISE AND SHIMMER

Varied thrushes wake me again this morning—is there any sweeter way to wake up?—and as thoughts steal in, I take pleasure in nudging them offstage so that I can resume enjoying the birds, along with the song of the creek. Half an hour later I am rescuing a mourning cloak butterfly from battering itself against the greenhouse walls. Nothing so easy as Gandalf catching the moth as he languished atop Saruman's tower, although almost as welcome a visitor.

It's hard to jump up and get busy in this place. Hard to impose my noises on the silence.

ISSUES

Even here, I have issues.

I have issues with the mosquitoes when they are abnormally large and behave like kamikazes, actually divebombing me. I wonder if they're attempting to scatter their competition: blackflies and no-see-ums.

Independence is a major issue. One breezy morning, I try to anchor the boat near shore so that I can scrape it at low tide. That fancy bottom paint is too expensive, so I have to scrape the barnacles off regularly, or gas prices will soar even higher and journeys will take longer and longer. All that growth causes drag. A truck and a trailer would get the boat out onto a ramp in town. This would almost be civilized. But I don't have a truck or a trailer, so I plan to beach the boat and scrape it one side at a time. It will take two full tide cycles.

Surely boat scraping is one of life's most hideous tasks. A boat's bottom is hard to get at no matter how you mount it. Gloves are ruined; hands become covered in cuts and scrapes; scraping tools break; barnacles are stuck fast and when they do come off, the gruesome mess is made worse by the knowledge that you are murdering thousands of innocents. Then you stink.

Last time, my buddy Phil anchored the boat. But on this breezy morning, I am alone. When I throw down the anchor, the bow swings around to face the shore instead of sitting parallel to it. Then the whole craft swings so that it will be sitting on top of the anchor when the tide goes out. After this happens several more times I try to retrieve the anchor. It's stuck under the neighbour's water line. After some struggle I raise it, look up and realize I'm almost grounded on the rocks. I look down. My hand is leaking blood and I have no idea why.

Eventually, I give up and bring the boat back to the float. I need a buddy not only to make the scraping job go more quickly, but to position the boat. I've failed. I'm a failure at independence today.

A small consolation is the thought that maybe independence isn't all it's chalked up to be. Nevertheless, it is something I crave almost as much as chocolate. My head aches. Can I somehow sneak into town, purchase some chocolate goodness and hurry back, tail between my legs? The bugger of it is, one trip would use up the whole tank. There's that much ecosystem thriving on the bottom of my boat. My barnacle colony.

HOLIDAY

As it happens, I am supposed to be on holiday, spending a week at the float without having to work shifts in town. I've never done such a thing before: spent an uninterrupted week in the Hang Loose Zone of no makeup, jewellery or restrictive garments. I've been looking forward to permanent hat-head, dirty fingernails, whiffy socks, nothing but the most unflattering clothes. But so far, it's no holiday. There was the boat ordeal, then the bugs, now the eighteen five-by-four windows that need cleaning, along with the usual lack of beer or hot showers, and the accidents.

I guess on any floathouse the potential for minor accidents is higher than in "normal" homes. But I think this one's got as many threats per inch as a construction zone in the city. There are rusty nails sticking up, loose, slippery ropes, a heavy solar panel with a long wire to trip over, gaps between planks, unattached ramps, an unbalanced dock that's sinking, a broken stairwell and low ceilings.

During this "holiday," I have bashed my forehead in the bedroom doorway, tripped over two ropes and the solar panel wire, nearly ripped off a nail, dropped the panel on my toe, stubbed the same toe in a gap and fallen no fewer than three times, though thankfully *not* into the cold, cold ocean. I want to eat chocolate cheesecake and wallow in chocolate mousse. Instead, I lie in my hammock and try not to touch anything.

VISITORS' QUESTIONS I CAN'T ALWAYS ANSWER

"What's that fish?"

"How many fish in a school?"

"How deep is the water here?"

"What does a jellyfish eat?"

"Is it dead or just asleep?"

"What kind of tree is that?"

"What is the prevailing wind speed and direction?"

"How much slack do you give the ropes?"

"How much gas do you go through in a week?"

PARADISE?

Come back in a November rainstorm when water pours through that one last leak that just won't fix, because it only drips when the wind blows the rain through a particular crack. Come back when the wind breaks the feeble old windows. When earplugs can't bring sleep due to the banging and pelting and squeaking and groaning of boat and dock and tires and ropes and floats and deck furniture. When it sounds like I'm in the middle of a car wash. When I'm washing the salt spray off the windows for the umpteenth time. When I feel woozy just trying to sweep the moving floor. When my handwriting looks as though I'm on a bus.

What to Do with Poo

My sister Kathy lives in Richmond along a busy street. It occurs to her one day to ask if there's an outhouse on board my floating home.

"Well, no," I say.

"Do you go on shore, then?"

"No, the ocean can cope with a tiny bit of pee."

There's a pause. Then it clicks.

"You mean you hang your butt off the side?"

"Exactly."

"But what about the neighbours?"

"There is only one neighbour," I tell her, "and we are hidden from each other by a peninsula."

"Well," she snickers, "you must be a fine sight."

Suddenly another thought strikes her. "What about number two?"

I decide to lead her into this one gradually. "Do you remember I told you we had a composting toilet at our other place? Well, we sold it and now we just use a bucket and compost it with sawdust as before. There's a lovely view—"

"YOU WHAT?!" she screams. She's laughing so hard she's wheezing. I hold the receiver away from my ear.

"I CAN'T BELIEVE—YOU MEAN YOU SHIT INTO A BUCKET! HA HA HA ..."

I have to explain. "But it's just the same as the old toilet except you roll it instead of turning the barrel! We put a nice comfy seat on it. What's the difference?"

She's calmed down somewhat now. "It just seems so primitive!"

"But Kathy, the entire town of Tofino flushes its raw sewage into the ocean. In fact, so does Victoria."

She can't believe this either. "In this day and age?"

"That's what I say."

"But ... what do you do when it gets full?" she giggles.

"Start another bucket," I say. I seize the opportunity to rave about another reason to be in love with our little Tofino library, which now has a book on composting poo, *The Humanure Handbook: A Guide to Composting Human Manure*. Written and self-published by J.C. Jenkins (1994), it is the funniest book ever. With chapter titles like "Crap Happens," "Deep Shit," "A Day in the Life of a Turd," "The Tao of Compost" and "The End is Near," you know you're in for a good read. And the photos, cartoons and diagrams along with the jam-packed-with-information text lets you in on the world of a family that really has their shit together.

Contemplating Rocks

How many hundreds of times have I let my kayak drift toward the creek? Yet this time I see some rocks I've never noticed before. A trio, fit together as if someone has had a hand in it. Two supports lidded by a big capstone covered with moss and a few nodding ferns, just like a prehistoric European burial chamber, or cromlech. All on a much smaller scale, of course. The structure is positioned between impenetrable forest, which crowds the stones, and open shoreline, where I sit in my kayak staring, feeling as though I'm being pulled toward the dark miniature doorway between them that draws my gaze.

Pipefish

Days later, again in the kayak, I drift near the float. A female kingfisher is using the roof's solar panel as a diving perch. She points like a spear at the water, so I think she'll slice through it noiselessly, but she splashes. A cute little splash, followed by a chattering—full-mouthed with wriggling fish or not. Meanwhile, an otter is gargling under the greenhouse. Yes, gargling.

In a minute they are both gone and I stare aimlessly at the water. A garter snake swims in an undulating S, slowly, scattering fish, and pauses to float in the sun before heading to shore. Here is a loose tuft of eel grass: four blades together. A pipefish darts out of the darkness to blend with the grass, perhaps fleeing from my enormous long shadow. Carefully I grasp one end of the clump, so we can't drift apart. A quarter of an hour later I am still engrossed in watching the fish as it curves its long graceful tail around a blade, moving along from end to end the same way we humans do on a pleasant afternoon stroll— except that when the fish changes direction, it darts, using a tiny fin. Its minute round eyes give way to a long, slim snout like its sea horse cousins'. And as their cousins do, the female transfers her eggs to the male's brood pouch where they will stay for weeks until it splits, releasing the tiny babies.

I try several times to touch the pipefish. Finally it toodles away.

I wonder if it was interacting with me. If it knew it was being watched.

TREASURE

The chives' flower heads have dried up and their black seeds are showing. I'm clearcutting the huge clumps, which I keep in the garden to distract pests from more prestigious plants. I slice through segments of each clump with a handsaw, the oniony scent making my eyes sting and water. I uncover something unexpected, exotic, beautiful. I gasp, throw the saw away and cup this new gift in my hands. A pale swallowtail butterfly, wings outstretched. It is wider than my palm, with black stripes on yellow, orange and blue near the tail.

Outside the greenhouse I open my hands next to the blooming sweet william. The insect remains on my palm, its long black proboscis curled up, poised above its splayed legs. Gently I nudge the butterfly toward the flowers and it clambers on, unwinding its proboscis and plunging it deep into the fragrant pink blossoms.

A while later I'm getting a sunburn watching the swallowtail contentedly probing as an infrequent breeze triggers those gorgeous wings to flutter. Soon I am forced to retreat from the sun. I read that this swallowtail, like many others, is often found sipping water at puddles. It must have been thirsty in my dry greenhouse. The caterpillars spin silken mats on leaves and then curl the leaves into shelters. One day I found a fat green guy curling up in a pink cosmos flower. This sounds beautiful, but my precious basil plants are full of holes made by these voracious caterpillars.

WEALTH

I love the essay in Kathleen Dean Moore's *Riverwalking* about a desert trip she takes with her family.[41] They carefully record many of the plants and all of the animals they find; even the children eagerly take part. Life, this planet, so rich: even in the desert. Like here: the greenhouse full of bees, the hummers quarrelling, the thrush sending up spiral after spiral punctuated by a flycatcher's quick three-syllable whistle, the song of a robin, distant, on the edge of my hearing; a megasunstar embracing a rope, its legs thick as a child's arms. A new sound grows fast and alarming, almost like an aircraft descending on me. An eagle is diving all the way from its favourite high perch on the other side of the bay. Bald eagles are said to possess a visual acuity eight times that of humans. This one can see the thousands of fish surrounding the float, and must be aware of me as well. My eyes aren't that acute, but my ears fill with the sound of wings cutting through air at high speed. The fish scatter, the eagles' legs—brown pantaloons over yellow talons—splay out crazily and stab at the water. *Spread-eagled*. It retreats with its catch to a boulder and swallows the fish whole, one quick gulp.

---

41   Kathleen Dean Moore, *Riverwalking: Reflections on Moving Water* (Boston: Houghton Mifflin Harcourt, 2001).

BRING ON THE NIGHT

It starts with sunset. A zigzag wisp of cloud by the camel-hump hill turns peach, radiating such a glow I could bite into the air and it would taste sweet. Everything becomes One Colour; I swear my face becomes peach, changes essential pigment, for one electrified moment. Then the blue between the wisp and the forest turns psychedelic turquoise.

I crouch on the edge of my deck an hour after dusk, swirling the biolume in tepid water with one hand while looking up at the stars. I've just finished whispering to myself, "The glory of the night," when a bat careens past my face. I hear the faint clicking of its wings as it makes a few more boomerang circles around the house, radaring for insects. How cruel that beauteous Night brings sleepiness.

Around eleven, I decide to go for a drift but leave the lights on in the house so that I can see how cozy it looks from a distance on the dark water. Paddling out into the bay stirs up the biolume as I go, far enough to see both floathouses, mine and my neighbour's. Two little lights all but engulfed in the night, minuscule under the starred, magnificent sky. Five stars (okay, meteors) fall in as many minutes. Soon I will stand up in the hot tub and come face to face with the eerie waning moon as it rises up behind the greenhouse.

Later I will hover on the edge of slumber and wake when a seal suddenly surfaces closer than it ever would in daylight, drawing a breath so deep yet sharp that my dreamy self believes the whole bay has been inhaled.

BIG BEAR

The bear must have heard my boat buzz into the bay, must have caught the sound of my motor being raised. But he or she just keeps crashing through the bushes until a massive black head emerges, framed with leaves, a head complete with fluorescent orange plastic tag enveloping one ear, torn green tag attached to the other.

It stands and pulls a branch of berries to its face. It drops and tears up a fern with its teeth. It is so big and bulky that it has to move slowly, and seems to stumble frequently on the rocky shore. It moves carefully, almost sulkily, yet resigned—as if each trudging step carries a sigh. Is it elderly? Full of old wounds?

Hot sun on black fur. The bear lowers itself into the water and just stays there for a while, cooling off. Then, slowly, so slowly, swims away. Every so often it makes a meagre attempt to crawl out, but it can't win over gravity and soon disappears around a bend, pursued by a teasing raven.

I have debates with friends on whether or not a swimming bear would dare climb aboard the floathouse. Old Tag-ear clearly couldn't have done so. There is no sloping surface. Could a young, nimble one?

More Dreaming

1. I lose the floathouse in rush-hour traffic, downhill, on a highway outside Nanaimo.

2. Someone has pulled everything (cabin, docks, greenhouse) uphill into the forest. It's a beautiful clearing, and I think: "Well, nice, but …" and look down to the naked water where my home was. A crew of workmen are towing a huge work site in, where they will build a resort or something industrial. "NO!" I cry, and the men all look up at me, and I am ashamed, because they are shaking their heads, muttering, "That one, she's against everything."

In Tune?

During the day, I think of nighthawks. Wonder about them. Will they appear again this year, and if so, when? That very evening their calls pierce the sky. This has happened to me at other times, with other species.

Do humans have a seasonal memory beneath consciousness? I'd like to think so. It could mean that we do belong here after all. That even if we lost everything we've built—computers, libraries, books, paper and pencils—and had no way to keep records, keep track, maintain calendars, know when, we might have an inner sensor or aerial waiting to stir awake and fine-tune itself. Then we'd understand the migration of birds and whales. We'd know why male rufous hummingbirds return south in June instead of October. But I don't want to wait until we lose all our technologies before getting into harmony with the natural world. Maybe we can have both, right now.

AN EVENING ON THE PENINSULA

Layers of rippling mountains darken in the shadow of a scarlet sunset. Closest to the water lies a layer of dark blue-grey, so comforting and cool after the long glare of summer day and blast of sea planes. That darkness seeps in, a distant peace, palpable yet mysterious. I know my floathouse is nestled in a snug cove far up the inlet, but can it be so? Do I really live inside this untouchable vision?

Unseen, there are pockets and bays breaking up the smooth dream of mountains and islands, the serene boundary of blue-grey, sealing sea from sky. There, a community of solitary floathouses. Here and there, homes embraced by water and forest. And exposed to storms.

Summer nights are blissful; mornings may be hugged by fog. In winter we long for the dipping and reaching mountains to ease the winds, take rests between rainfall, break open the sky between storms for more than a day.

In the forest at Tonquin Park off Tofino is a deep, round pool, a metre across, cedar-brown water, the only stillness in a rushing stream. A point of division—the stream splits into two opposing directions. Surrounded by dense salal bushes, its source hidden, untrackable, untraceable. Light foam moves over the water, and a single fern frond reaches from the far bank to rest its tips on the surface like fingers. There, foam gathers, sticking to the spores underneath. The edge of the pond pours over a stump that looks petrified. I stand in water, in gumboots and rainpants even though the stream as it makes for the beach is shallow, tumbling over rocks until meeting smooth sand. There it re-forms: artery shapes in the sand, rearranging billions of grains into something like art. Lapping at the sand like a snake's tongue.

Veins of the planet. Sacred water, mysterious source. I never come here without gumboots, so that my desire to be part of the stream can always be fulfilled. Between stream, ocean waves and rocks that guard the forest is a stretch of smooth, wet sand, soft and shiny like a whale's belly. Such sleekness defies the dramatic weather and its effect on moving water. I leave the stream and let my boots sink into the grey flesh.

The tide sweeps in, chases me and my footprints away. There isn't any beach left to walk on, or sink into. I rejoin the boardwalk in the forest, seeking the huge cedar tree that seems to have carved a place for itself out of the surrounding air. Old cedars eventually leave a cake-fork impression of themselves, as if they're trying to impale the sky. Nothing brown about their trunks; they're as grey as December. The greenishness about them is from all the different plants, bushes, ferns and tree seedlings growing upon/from them. This Tonquin tree is no different. Recently I discovered I could spot it plainly from the beach: a stark, stone grey hulk amid the green of the forest, its top one of many sword-tip snags, a telltale sign of old growth. On the boardwalk I stand and gaze up at it, then move on to the evergreen huckleberry bushes. It's winter and I'm eating berries. They're black with a maroon aura, small, very firm and not too sweet, but cold and juicy with a satisfying chewy texture. A memory of late summer bursts in my mouth. Berries in December. I think of Briony Penn, who raves about berry picking and how it allows her stomach to be filled with local fruit, "instead of the fruit of yet another banana republic."[42]

THERE GOES MY GREENHOUSE

A long time ago I was partnered, but he was away. I was staying in town, and the power went out for three hours—a familiar occurrence in windy winter conditions. I told myself that, come morning, I must call our floating neighbour, a busy, no-nonsense, white-bearded fellow, and ask him to check on our place.

I wasn't out of bed yet when the neighbour called me from his radio phone. (This was before the invasion of cellular phones.)

"Chris? It's Mike. Your greenhouse float has broken away and is drifting. I can see it from here. Over."

"Oh, no. Over."

"I'm in a hurry to get to work. You'd better find someone to help you. Over."

"But you won't leave it loose, will you, Mike? I know nothing about anchor lines and all this stuff. Over."

"I'll go have a look, but I don't have much time. Out."

I didn't hear from him, nor see his boat come in to town, for an hour and a half. In the meantime I wasn't going to go rounding people up until I knew what the situation was. Instead, I phoned my partner in Bella Coola and asked him to come home.

"Aren't you sorry we ever moved onto this titanic nightmare?" I whined.

When I finally met with Mike in town, the news was good and bad. "I've got it secured pretty good," he said. "But it's really just temporary. A piece of deck is gone. I found your kayak way up the creek."

"And the solar panels?" I asked.

---

42   Briony Penn, "Huckleberry August: Chaos and Harmony in the Classic Patch," in *A Year on the Wild Side*.

"What solar panels?"

"Oh, no."

Mike drew a diagram of the floats and how they had been tied to shore. He tried to explain how they *should* be tied. The house was fine; it was the greenhouse float that caused the problems. It was heavy and insecurely anchored, and that made the entire setup vulnerable to big gusts. My precious garden needed to be stabilized properly by someone who knew what she or he was doing, and then the house tied to it, rather than the greenhouse tied to the house. The diagram with its loops and arrows got more and more complex. It looked like the drawing of a disturbed child or a mad artist's design.

I cycled around town looking for the guy Mike had recommended for the job. Left notes on bulletin boards. Listened to the marine forecast. Gale warning, of course. Highly unstable. New frontal systems moving in, one after the other.

My partner came home; we dealt with the crisis. Found a diver who had experience with anchors, floathomes, aquaculture, underwater photography, you name it. Since that day there have been many more storms. Divers are well employed around here.

Drama Queen

The sun has been my focal point all day, dictating where and how often I move things: my body, plants, the solar panel. It sinks behind the Cone, its departure momentous. Suddenly I'm standing, arms reaching up to it, and I'm launching into the song Annie Lennox sings at the end of the *Lord of the Rings* movie trilogy. Nobody sees or hears me. There's something about white gulls crying on the horizon across the sea ... A pale moon rising, ships coming to carry you home ... Souls passing as light on the water. Something like that. I sing in an imperfect voice to the disappearing sun, the bereft sky, the silent forest, the secretive water.

In Pursuit

On September 8, 2013, a young, thin cougar attacked a woman in her garden on Flores Island. I don't know her well, but the times I've chatted with her I've been struck by her friendliness. Her husband fought the cougar with a spear, and it retreated. Conservation officers found its body.

Trauma, bravery, resilience, the long road of recovery, grief.

PART 2
ASPHALT SEASON

Escape From The Slide Parties

It's safe to write about this now, while the male hummingbirds are zooming in to tongue the luscious pink columbines. Safely early spring. Safer than midsummer, when the peas are already dying. Safer certainly than late summer, when even the female hummers have abandoned me in pursuit of a stronger sun, their sugar-water feeders hanging useless and forlorn.

Now that the wild rose bushes are full of pastel pink, fragrant blooms, the encroaching darkness of October feels far away, unworthy of concern. Poor, berated and maligned darkness.

Nevertheless.

In the dead of winter I get the small-town blues. I can't seem to get out of bed before ten in the morning. The sky is grey and so is my face. When I first wrote this my town boasted three main hangouts besides the beach, and in February the same people were always there, bless them. There is but one pub left. Many of the restaurants close for at least part of the winter. Scary times: you cannot hide, unless you disappear into the wide wilderness, and you need a boat to get there. But at this time of year, it's anonymity I crave, and less isolation, not more. I long for ethnic meals, a night out; my body longs to dance. Live music, charming pubs, pulsing nightclubs. My brain yearns for stimulation. Alternative radio, live poetry, museums, art shows, and did I mention the dancing that so purringly kindles one's brain?

Three or four city days fill me up with culture. I know I've reached saturation when I retire at night feeling grimed, the traffic noise bothers me, I miss seeing familiar faces and wonder what the gossip is back home. Not to mention that my bank balance is wearing thin. One last trip to second-hand bookstores to soak up the atmosphere, and I prepare for the return trip. But before I leave, maybe I'll shoot some slides.

Slide parties are a quaint example of Tofino's winter nightlife. No, I don't mean parties held in children's playgrounds. Slide *show* parties. The host provides the screen and projector, sets up, shows some of her own slides and hopes others bring theirs. It's a pastime, and not a bad one the first few occasions. There's never anything bleak and haunting like ruins of the Orkney isles or standing stones in the Yorkshire heath, a brooding Brontë landscape. Someone always brings Mexico slides, and everyone oohs and ahhs at the dusty palm trees, the dried-up brown grasses, the grimy city streets and markets full of mangos and papayas. We partygoers moan about rain and swear we'll be on the next air-polluting plane to some third-world country where we can't drink the water.

One resident likes to bring slides of himself naked in beautiful settings, usually around Clayoquot. There he is, running through the waves on a wild beach on Flores Island, splashing so that the water perfectly (and luckily) covers his privates. Or riding away on his bike with the outgoing tide, goosebumps glowing in the sunset. These provide a break from the host's many close-up slides of locals as they were ten or fifteen years ago—pictures that can frankly be painful.

I'm inclined to sulk through these events, but a recent party provided a reasonable mix. Palm trees and hammocks, kayak trips, BC mountain hike vistas, Russia/the Soviet Union in 1978, and the town pot activist's India slides. This individual had uncovered an India full of naked men with dreadlocks, their bodies smeared with ashes, sitting smoking hashish or standing stretching their penises with sticks.

Don't get me wrong, I love Tofino in winter. It's quiet (except for the floatplanes), not crowded; mild and green. The storms make for great surf and exciting power outages (hopefully not during a slide party). I actually prefer it to summer, when it closely resembles a city—only *without* the IMAX theatres, alternative radio, live poetry, nightclubs and malls.

Of course, Victoria and Vancouver aren't big or new enough sometimes. Since I used to live across the Atlantic, the craving to go back periodically stirs, and if there's money, I do. As a rule, for longer than three or four days.

⋙

Glasgow in January: the Celtic Connections music festival is on, so I'm out every night, bypassing the Euro Hostel's malfunctioning lift to hop down nine flights of stairs (I have an irritable ankle). Alone. Groups of younger Glaswegians trail between nightclubs, the women's skirts so high the glacial wind is surely entering their wombs. Is this why these same women, running the shops by day, are so unfriendly when I go in to shop or browse? On Vancouver Island we in retail—without fail— will greet you with a smile, ask you how you are, demand to know if we can help you and press you to have a great day. In Glasgow, it is the security guards (every shop has them) who become my friends.

Red double-decker buses are torrenting down narrow rainwashed streets. On the wrong side. I love this. After the evening's scheduled concert performance I chance the clubs, as long as a venue doesn't prohibit entry to those over thirty (actual policy in some places). There are hundreds to explore, overwhelming to someone from a one-bar town. A jovial pair of geezers offers to take me to a pub frequented by locals and I accept. I never would have found it on my own, and we have a bonny time. The sign says, "THE SCOTIA BURNS SPECIAL. Cock-a-leekie Soup and Haggis, Neeps & Tatties, £3.50." The city is alive with all ages and my perma-grin is back, until this happens the very

PHOTO WARREN RUDD.

next night: I visit a metal club and excuse myself for accidentally nudging a lass. Snickering, she replies, "That's all right, Granma."

I'm barely forty-one and don't look it. Certainly don't act it. Much later I remember a Nomeansno CD cover showing graffiti on the outside wall of some punk-show venue in an unknown city. It reads, "HOW FUCKEN OLD ARE NOMEANSNO? GIVE IT UP GRAND DADS" [sic]. Underneath, in smaller writing, the band's drummer has retorted: "THAT'S 'GREAT GRAND DAD' TO YOU, FUCKER!—JOHN WRIGHT."

Later, in Canada, I lie and tell everyone that I turned back to my fellow metal clubber and hissed, "That's 'Great Granma' to you, fucker!"

The night after my encounter with ageism I go to a second metal club and meet Austin, a bonny lad who makes me forget all about "Granma." And I get my fifth tattoo, a very small, green Celtic knot on my upper arm, from a nice lass around the corner from the hostel.

When the festival is over I fly to Amsterdam to visit friends. Snow is falling on this beautiful city. Before leaving for Italy I get lost at night and am struck with a wave of homesickness.

In the Paris train station I become disoriented and nearly miss my connection. After leaping onto a moving train I frantically rummage in my bag—for what? I don't even consciously know. Until I find it, my hand closing around a small stone from Frank Island on Chesterman Beach. Relief floods me, my breathing normalizes and I feel grounded, connected to home, familiarity, belonging. The stone remains gripped in my fist for the rest of the day.

I ride several more trains to Italy, a place I've dreamed of all my life. In Milan, before I can say "No thank you," men are tying thread bracelets around my wrists, and they want payment for them. I lose count of the hundreds of pointed spires on the cathedral, or in proper Italian, the *duomo*. This building is like a gothic orgasm, completely over the top. I remember seeing a slide of it for the first time, in high school, thrilled anyone had the nerve to build such a place. I pay eight Euros to ride the lift to the roof, where there are even more pinnacles. The interior is surprisingly dark. I later feast my eyes on Leonardo's *The Last Supper* inside the markedly ungothic *refettorio* of Chiesa di S. Maria delle Grazie. Truly, this is worlds away from scruffy Vancouver Island.

Starting a new day at my hostel, both the men's and women's dorms are robbed just before dawn. Nearly everyone loses valuables. I am the only one in my dorm unscathed, because I sleep every night with my bag that holds cash, cards and passport. A German senior tells me it is her second visit to Italy and that she was robbed both times. She laughs shakily. "Do I blame this country, or myself?" I sit with her awhile as people line up to report their stolen items.

I find a temporary companion: twenty-one-year-old Amanda from California. She has already lived in Spain and seeks tutoring and nanny work. On her laptop she writes about her mother, whom she has only known a couple of years. We share some laughs in a dark, cowboys-and-Indians-themed pub called the Sitting Bull. The toilet is a hole in the floor! Amanda has had worse days than I have this trip. The night before a job interview she was kicked out of her accommodations for refusing to sleep with the landlord; on the train she realized she'd left her laptop at his place. A child in the next seat puked on her. Leaving the station, she fell down some stairs. I'm not sure how the job interview turned out.

So many elderly street people in Milan. One man prostrates himself across the sidewalk, nearly off the curb, hands pressed together as if in prayer, truly begging in the literal sense. A woman seems to be sitting on the piazza pavement with her legs out in front of her, but in fact they are bent the wrong way.

On my own again, I crick my neck studying residential balconies adorned with Romanesque arches and draped in vines or enhanced by potted palms. Everything feels ancient in a way different from trees. Later I write in a poem, "Crumbling opulence under a sun gone nova / : Milano."[43] I'm thinking it feels like Charn, a ruined city where Polly and Digory find the queen Jadis in C.S. Lewis's *The Magician's Nephew*.

I find the Natural History Museum in a park and am frustrated by the trees. Leafless, unidentifiable. Admission is free because it is Charles Darwin Day. There are the usual dead mounted insects, beautiful moths and butterflies, fossils—but also huge displays of crystals, some so *far out* it's hard to imagine they came out of this planet. Next I take to wandering smaller roads, which are unbelievably quiet for such a large city, and winding. Some are so narrow they are claustrophobic, and I begin to resent how the buildings shut out the sun.

When I get the chance to check my email, there's a message from my well-travelled friend Osprey. She tells me to "suck it up" regarding my homesickness. I am going to call my poem "Always the Reluctant Traveller." Outside the train's windows roll gentle hills, valleys, rivers, villages. I move south in the sun, as toward spring, another reason besides loneliness to be home. For now, though, surely I must continue achieving lifelong travel goals.

In Florence I could almost lick the candied architecture. I stop and stare at it like every other tourist. The interior of the lip-smacking duomo is seven hundred years of condensed spaciousness and peace. I mellow more with every visit. Many years ago while working full-time

---

43   Christine Lowther, "Always the Reluctant Traveller," in *My Nature*.

in Canterbury I'd spent every lunch hour in the cathedral grounds. Great cathedrals deserve multiple visits, and religion has nothing to do with it. My dodgy knee worsens climbing 415 steps to the top of the Campanile di Giotto, a rectangular tower beside the duomo. Determined to do everything, I also climb the cathedral dome itself; not only are there more steps, they're steeper and narrower. A tight, vertigo-inducing balcony goes all the way around the inside of the dome so that all the lowly sinners can get a close look at the frescoes. Especially those fun-in-hell scenes: sinners being fed to the fires or devoured by demons. What would ancient religious leaders think if they knew Michelangelo's *David*'s genitals are now emblazoned on men's shorts for sale in street markets? What would the artist himself think?

Not far away in the Galleria dell'Accademia, the real and whole sculpted *David* won't keep still. Like other great works of sculpture, he moves. Even the white marble of him flickers into skin tones ...

The dramatic approach to *David* is through a hall filled with Michelangelo's unfinished or emerging slaves. Every slave is worth hours of study. But he, *David*, is so purely magnificent, complete. Through a small glass dome, natural light falls down onto his huge head, that mass of wavy hair, and onto his shoulders. He stands high on a plinth, in sensuous contrapposto. He used to stand with those statues outside the Uffizi Gallery, more accessible to the people; now he is protected from the elements. I am sitting on the bench behind him when, for a nanosecond, his skin changes from cream to flesh and he begins, ever so slightly, to move. A guard then shouts "NO PHOTO" to some students near me and breaks the spell.

There is, of course, much more to Florence: Fra Filippo Lippi's exquisite paintings; Botticelli's *The Birth of Venus*; the river Arno; Michelangelo's and Galileo's tombs and Giotto's frescoes in the Franciscan Basilica di Santa Croce, which also has an oddly placed, rare recycling bin in its peaceful cloisters; how a shop clerk finds me the one microwavable vegan soup possibly in all of Italy (hostels here don't offer kitchen use); how I use Skype for the first time here. Santa Croce also houses the sculpture that inspired New York's Statue of Liberty, and this one symbolizes the liberty of poetry! Ageism turns me off a trip to Pisa: every hostel I research has a young age limit.

In Rome the open-topped double-decker stops next to orange trees. The fruit is within my reach but I'm afraid to pick it in case it's infused with street pollution. Or in case someone yells at me like I'm a student in a gallery, raising a camera to my face. Or maybe I can't believe my eyes, and think these can't be real oranges if they're not on display in a supermarket. I'm surprised jars of Nutella don't grow on trees, the stuff is so popular here, while I cannot find peanut butter.

It's February, and the days are mainly sunny but chilly in the shade. Rome is huge, crammed, chaotic and noisy. The gaudy, clotted baroque cream of San Pietro drips decoration. I follow an enormous wall all the way around Vatican City and pay fourteen Euros entry! I run past great works, weave in and out of courtyards and museums, along corridors hung with tapestries of ancient maps, under ceilings of gold, through sumptuously decorated halls past signs warning me not to slip and fall down steps. I quickly photograph Raphael's *School of Athens*.

Finally I reach the Sistine Chapel, which I studied as a student in art history a million years ago. The wall showing Judgment Day has been restored to its original bright blue, and the entire chapel is richly coloured. It is busy with hundreds of figures in Biblical scenes. Visitors crane their necks to gaze up at the fall of Adam and Eve. My neck is permanently sore. Michelangelo was obsessed with rendering the beauty and strength of the human body; here he was given free reign. I appreciate it all as much as I can, but the Old Testament was inescapably misogynist. I will leave here ready to seek out plenty of woman-positive art and a return to my pagan roots.

My eye keeps seeking the balm of a magnificent female figure holding a huge open book. She is typical of Michelangelo's painted personages only in being muscular and not thin. Her arms are a body builder's. Her calves, I am pleased to note, are huge. She has her back to us, but is turning toward profile, full of grace, humility and strength. I ask an attendant about this painting, and he names her in his rich accent: The Libyan Sibyl, prophetess. The first woman to chant oracles. She who foretold the "coming of the day when that which is hidden shall be revealed."

My own inner Sibyl (a freckled redhead in tartan canvas hightops) foresaw that this might happen: a change of loosely made plans. There is no friend or companion with whom to marvel, and I'm sick of travelling on my own. This señorita doesn't go clubbing anymore. She misses the over-friendly west coast; the bubble of belonging that is her lack-of-nightlife village. All is forgiven.

It was winter when I left. It is winter when I return (a month early). But not for long.

I post my trip pictures in albums on Facebook after manically researching and copying information online about each feature and monument. Slide shows have given way to PowerPoint presentations or, again, Facebook. Those informal, technologically quaint parties don't seem to be a part of Tofino winters anymore. Or it may be that my ambivalent attitude toward them gets in the way of invitations.

Five and a half years later my *David* fridge magnets (not that I have a fridge) are in good shape, but my prized postcard reproduction of Sibyl is looking well-loved.

Generally Giving a Damn

After surveying all the possibilities available to them—God, sports, drugs and booze, conforming to the culture around them—they had chosen punk. Punk made sense to these girls; it was one of the only things that did.

—Sara Marcus,
Girls to the Front: The True Story of the Riot Grrrl Revolution

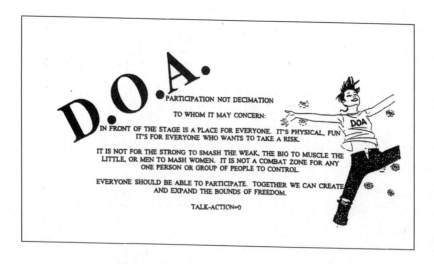

Katrina leaps from the stage, and a cornfield of willing hands carries her safely away. "This song is called 'General Strike,'" announces singer Joey Shithead, and I scream with joy. Suddenly I'm away from the stage, in the centre of the pit, big guys all around me, gals too: elbows, knees, muscles, boots; theirs, mine. I feel no fear. I am ecstatic.

I'm five foot two; my friend Katrina is even shorter. Right now she has a bloody nose and is going for yet another stage dive. I stay put at the front of the stage, my hips already bruised by constantly getting mashed up against it. Both Katrina and I have blazing-wide perma-grins on our faces. We're at a D.O.A. show.

What year is it? 1984? '85? How old am I? Seventeen?

Oh, right. It's August 20, 2011. I am in my forties. Katrina's what, thirty-five? But in this moment I am not thinking of age, aging, or age-lessness. I might not even remember my own name.

The first time I went to a punk show I was in grade twelve. My friend Jodi took me on the bus over Second Narrows bridge to see a band called D.O.A. They sang a song called "Fucked Up Ronnie." It was about US president Ronald Reagan. Here was a band unafraid of finger pointing or the naming of corrupt politicians, a band singing loudly of class inequality, a band—one of many, as it turned out—brave enough to say "Fuck you." To say I was hooked was the un-derstatement of 1984. Jodi said I spent the whole gig with eyes and mouth wide open.

After that Jodi and I went to gigs every weekend possible. We shared classes at school and would scour the concert pages of the *Georgia Straight* while we were supposed to be doing classwork. We could only attend all-ages shows, of which there were plenty. We had to leave shows in time for the last bus back to the North Shore.

Canadian prime minister Brian Mulroney cancelled the youth program Katimavik, leaving me dangling at the end of grade twelve with no Plan B. Conservative governments held sway over Canada, the States and the United Kingdom. In the first few years of high school I'd been immersed in the peace movement, listening to a lot of flower-child music. But even though rock was supposedly rebel music, it didn't fit with the anger I felt at Mulroney, Reagan, British prime minister Margaret Thatcher and their nuclear arms race that kept me up at night.

Why wasn't anyone singing with honest rage and fear?

According to the 2011 film *Bloodied But Unbowed*, punks from elsewhere thought of Vancouver as "a hotbed of protest" with a "huge anarchist movement."[44] Too many bands south of the border wrote about wanting girls and drugs—just like mainstream rock. In contrast, Vancouver band lyrics were often about exposing injustices. Local group Unnatural Silence had a song about the 1945 US atomic bombing of Hiroshima, and Shanghai Dog's "American Desert" was about the US testing of atomic blasts on its own military personnel. That's not to say there weren't some inspiring US bands too—like the Dead Kennedys, Fugazi, M.D.C. and Reagan Youth—but this was a time before the web, so I was immersed in the scene of my own city. Though I loved the occasion of bands coming from out of town, I formed a loyalty to the locals.

This immersion included our experimentations with the anti-fashions (Jodi preferred pointed, buckled goth footwear while I stuck to steel-toed combat boots). Then there were the zines (pronounced "zeens"), an alternative to magazines. These were cut-and-paste affairs, printed on photocopiers and bursting with gig and record reviews, as well as band interviews and political, anarchist, feminist and animal rights diatribes. We started our own and called it *Cheeky Rebel*. This was in honour of my Gram, who so often complained that I was cheeky.

Once a month I'd lay out announcements for rallies and marches and let flow my opinions, rants and poems on nukes, American warships in our city's harbour, school, posers, BC's Social Credit government, public transit, war, Expo 86, religion, getting kicked out of the house for having purple hair, sexism, the Nanoose Bay military base, TV or violent movies. Jodi excelled at gig reviews. Neither of us had computers at home—hardly anyone did yet—so I typed on a borrowed

---

44   *Bloodied But Unbowed*, directed by Susanne Tabata (Tabata Productions, 2011).

or school keyboard. Once in a while Beth or a friend would offer artistic smidgens but mostly we'd clip and paste silly headlines from ultra-religious rags or reproduce band logos. *Cheeky Rebel* was work, even at just a single legal-size sheet folded in half to make four sides. But it was our baby. What glee we felt as our monthly creation came together, even if it was over a photocopier prone to jamming. I think the most exciting interview we scored was with Chris Crud, a total sweetheart who stage managed every gig in Vancouver. Before each band came on, Chris would run all over the stage hooking everything up and testing it. He knew a lot of bands. He told us that his worst gig experience was Scotland's the Exploited. "I swear I set up the drum kit thirty-six times," he told us.

We distributed *Cheeky Rebel* to all the alternative record and clothing stores downtown. It was the key to meeting punks and actually having people we knew to say hi to at gigs—a comfort zone via our own creation! As Sara Marcus wrote in her book *Girls to the Front*, "And having a zine to hand out made talking to strangers unbelievably easy. [You] could just go up to anyone—people a lot older than [you], and people in bands—and say, 'Want a zine?'"[45]

One of the things I loved about punk was that you didn't have to be good-looking to be cool. Rebellious, knowledgeable, busy, sure. But here, the tyranny of *pretty* was largely irrelevant. It was thrilling to be among so many long-time fellow outcasts.

Zine writers and readers wrote to each other in a vibrant exchange of opinions. Jodi and I quickly acquired pen pals. Packages came every day full of letters, pictures, posters, flyers. I learned about important issues never taught or even brought up in formal education, like vivisection and factory farms and slaughterhouses. I wanted to convert to vegetarianism, as many punks were doing, but didn't make the leap

45   Sara Marcus, *Girls to the Front: The True Story of the Riot Grrrl Revolution* (Harper Perennial, 2010).

until one night in 1986 at a Spores show at the New York Theatre on Commercial Drive. The lead singer was wrapped in cow entrails that reeked of formaldehyde.

When I went to college I moved from my Gram's on the North Shore to a so-called anarchist house in East Van. My boyfriend was a perfect gentleman named Barry who played guitar for a fuckband called New Heads and produced a zine called *The Happy Hobo*. The term "anarchism" attached to the house confused my eighteen-year-old self because everyone living there was expected to vote in elections at every level. My roommates, Steve, Julie and Nedjo, had given just about every *ism* more thought than I had, and they supported feminist political parties and green government. They knew that women had died to get Julie and me the right to vote.

Even though the voting requirement might not have followed anarchist principles, our house was run on them: sharing chores, holding weekly meetings, equality for all. It was also where a youth-run alternative newspaper, *Next Generation*, was produced. Nearly everybody who ever moved in ended up writing for it. I had submitted articles while still in high school and was excited to be dwelling in this hub, which attracted exciting visitors, like Gerry Hannah and Evelyn Lau.

My roommates were all a few years older than me—post-grad university students. I was the baby, dyeing, crimping and razoring my hair and not wanting to be left alone at night in the house; at gigs I had to watch out for a mohawked girl who liked to pick me up and throw me into the slam pit. We never actually spoke, but I was thinking of her when I wrote in *Cheeky Rebel*, "The people at gigs are on your side!" I like to think she was an exception—that women supported each other. Otherwise, how could we have had all-women groups like Animal Slaves or Industrial Waste Banned? It's too bad I hadn't heard Joe Strummer's statement, "Punk rock means exemplary manners to your fellow human being." I took comfort in the proudly feminist zine *Smarten UP!* produced by Jean Smith, the singer for Mecca Normal. I wrote to her—or did she write to me first? I don't remember, but we became fast friends, despite my awe of her. The summer of 2014 marked the thirtieth anniversary of her first gig, when the band opened for D.O.A. Jean posted on Facebook:

> Part of the idea for creating Mecca Normal was a reaction to the lack of women in bands in Vancouver. It definitely seemed like the guys were in the bands and the girls watched the guys. It was annoying. To me, starting a band demonstrated a solution to the issue. Luckily the idea caught on with the advent of Riot Grrrl in the 1990s.

Many of these people are my Facebook friends now: Jodi, Jean, Chris Crud, even Joe (Shithead) Keithley. Not the mohawked girl, and, unfortunately, not my old roommates. They probably don't approve of Facebook. I get that. But way out here at the end of the road I cherish connections. At the end of the 2011 D.O.A. performance, Katrina and I were dishevelled and deliriously happy; I recall that we stumbled out into the night and let the rain wash us clean. At a show like that, the world feels once again on the right track, and for one night I can forget my country is run—and being run over—by Stephen Harper, who almost makes Mulroney feel like a big teddy bear. Now in 2014 we don't know if Tofino will ever have another one like it. My inner punk goes hungry too much of the time. Perhaps I can be forgiven for looking back.

Once in a great while I still pore over old master copies of *Rebel* and am amazed at how good the scene was then, even for all-ages shows. I remember someone in *Bloodied But Unbowed* saying that Vancouver had an art scene that pushed us to be more creative and outrageous, birthing bands like I, Braineater (whose singer, Jim Cummins, I secretly lusted after). Imagine a lineup of AKOB (Another Kind of Blues), Death Sentence, San Francisco's all-gal Frightwig and England's GBH (Grievous Bodily Harm), all on one night. (Jodi's review: "Outstanding! Brilliant!") Imagine the York presenting Skinny Puppy on July 5, SNFU and Nomeansno on the sixth, and Bolera Lava on the seventh. Did those years really happen? Life had to have been good in Vancouver in 1985. Indeed, in August of 2013 my friend Dan Walters of the zine *Terminally Stupid* released an online photozine called *DIVING WITH YOUR BOOTS ON: 1985: The Year in Punk and Hardcore*. Dan writes of the joy he has in revisiting it now. I remember the wonder as I gaze upon hundreds of pictures of bands and their audiences, catching sight of myself looking immeasurably young and dorky in a mullet.

In 1986 I started corresponding with the producer of England's *Direct Action* zine, an impressive publication of many pages. Patrick McKernan was a bass player and writer in "Britain's fastest band," Atavistic. When I finally made it to England in July 1987, I stayed with him and his parents and sisters in Whitstable, a town near Canterbury. His mother served me a proper English tea.

Pat had interviewed the members of Crass, a band like no other. At eight minutes long, their song "Nagasaki Nightmare" was a rebellion against punk mainstream. Crass sang for the working class, their music was revolutionary, their daily lives exemplary. Or so I thought. Later Pat told me that, though he once believed the sun shone out their behinds, he found them hypocritical and pretentious as hell.

I found UK punks both deeply class-aware and prone to criticizing each other. They opened my eyes to poverty issues and to dirty fingers in dirty pies. Some things I learned were disappointing. My guilty favourite, seemingly activist pop band, U2, were signed with Island, a record label distributed by EMI, a corporation involved in the production of guided missiles. I had thought Bob Geldof's Live Aid effort to relieve the Ethiopian famine was heroic. With Chumbawamba's revolutionary *Pictures of Starving Children Sell Records* LP, I saw the world needed more systemic change.

Pat informed me that many apparently vegetarian food products might contain animal fat, and that cheese itself, unless labelled "vegetarian," contained rennet, taken from the stomach lining of a calf. Besides, dairy and egg production could be as cruel as meat production. These facts were known and publicized by animal rights groups all over Britain, but Pat's knowledge and ethics especially stirred me. He had pen pals up and down the country and around the world. We travelled together, then moved in together and went vegan.

Pat and I also did a few issues of a new zine together, named *The Earth Cries Mi-Fa-Mi* after a poem of my mother's, but even though its subject matter was still good—body image, book and zine reviews, work, Sea Shepherd, women in the scene, poetry and lyrics—I didn't like it as much as *Cheeky Rebel* or *Direct Action*. It was tidy and mature, and like too many zines, you needed a magnifying glass to read the font. I went along on tour with Atavistic, and thought of my friend Jodi who, meanwhile, had become much cooler than me. She had learned bass guitar and joined and formed bands herself, and was playing gigs.

Early on in my British life, before moving in with Pat, I visited Greenham Common Women's Peace Camp and was shocked to see convoys of nuclear missile carriers—accidents waiting to happen—moving along the road right in front of me. In London, later on, my eyes were further widened at the poll tax riot. Pat and I watched people set the South African embassy on fire to protest apartheid. An ambulance almost ran someone over, or maybe it was a police van, and our friend Ted—there with his baby—went running zigzag, away into the crowd, pushing the pram before him at top speed. Horses were injured as police attempted equestrian crowd control. We couldn't leave, as every side street we legged down to find a tube station was blocked by the tendrils of chaos resulting from two hundred thousand fed-up citizens facing the old bill. Well, people were angry. The poll tax was cruel and Thatcher's rule seemed eternal. When the news broke that she had finally resigned I thought it was a joke.

The photographs I have of those years are from a small box camera whose *click* was more of a *clunk*. They are small, square colour prints kept in old albums in my floathouse loft. And right now several albums lie open all over the floor where I'm sitting. Why not, when it's storming outside and cozy inside? Here's a shot of me in those red and black tie-dyed tights I wore forever, soaked after walking for miles in the raining Kentish countryside for some cause. I wasn't chasing the fox hunt that time … I never could keep up with horses. My face looks like I was looking forward to getting inside somewhere cozy. I look up from my albums now: through the window is a wet, wind-blown duck who clearly doesn't mind such weather. It's happily feeding from one of my ropes. I remember being visited here by a couple of European punk squatters. They didn't miss hot water and a bathroom. Despite the mossy roof, unfinished ceilings, disrepair, and splintery floor, they thought my home was fantastic. I wonder if they'd've been as charmed in monsoon season. But they reminded me that before the provincial government cracked down on floaters, I was a kind of squatter too.

> I was not yet sure where my political affinities lay, but I knew that I respected what the activists and punks were doing: taking old decrepit buildings and turning them into homes, creating community gardens, making their own newspapers and zines, and just generally giving a damn.

> —Isa Chandra Moskowitz[46]

46   Isa Chandra Moskowitz, *Vegan with a Vengeance: Over 150 Delicious, Cheap, Animal-Free Recipes That Rock* (Jackson, TN: Da Capo Press, 2005).

Pat and I used to visit our friends in the London squats. Some of them lived remarkably industrious lives in houses that had been abandoned or slated for demolition or gentrification. Once in a while bottom floors had to be sealed off because of rats, and sometimes other parts of the homes were unstable and dangerous. Most of the time, though, the buildings were sound, and people were able to live in them safely and comfortably. Anyway, it was a travesty houses should be empty when so many individuals were homeless (just like in Tofino). In *Talk-Action=0: An Illustrated History of D.O.A.*, Joe Keithley talks about his band's first European tour: "We were introduced to a whole other level of politics we had not seen or experienced in North America ... Squatters would take over abandoned buildings and turn them into productive centres that included art and performance venues, workshops, and living space."[47] In his book *I, Shithead: A Life in Punk*, he writes of "unused buildings turned into camps for refugees ... concert halls, bookstores, and best of all, gathering places for shit disturbers ... In many places the local governments gave up trying to evict the squatters and instead just gave them the buildings."[48]

Unfortunately my friends were not so lucky, but they hung on as long as they could. We knew a couple—he was a Brit; she, Italian—who ran a zine-distribution service from their squat, receiving and mailing hundreds of grassroots publications. They were at every gig, standing behind a table covered in alternative reading material. Another friend, Pete, pursued his studies from a squat, joined Reclaim the Streets, chased down fascist skinheads and started a hunt saboteurs group at the University of London. Pat's brother Robin moved in with Pete and followed his own callings of art and teaching.

---

47   *Joe Keithley, Talk-Action=0: An Illustrated History of D.O.A.* (Vancouver: Arsenal Pulp Press, 2011).

48   *Joe Keithley, I, Shithead: A Life in Punk* (Vancouver: Arsenal Pulp Press, 2003).

We loved to travel, and in the summer of 1989 Pat and I went to an international anarchist conference in San Francisco where we saw the Yeastie Girls perform. That was the first place and time I saw a man in a dress. How liberating! But it was always good to get back to Whitstable: then-population 25,000. The self-imposed pressure in big cities to be in with the coolest was too much for me by that time.

Meanwhile mohawks gave way to dreadlocks; there were myriad punk subcultures, at least in Britain. In Canterbury, where I worked in a health food store, many punks worked on the archeological digs, patiently brushing soil from skeletons in all weathers. Pat got a job there, as did our friend Max. Max's backyard was an animal sanctuary, full of rabbit runs plus a rampant goat named Bilbo. A small posse of us vegans would take Bilbo and Max's dog, Oz, for walks in the nearby woods, a place blanketed with bluebells in spring. We called ourselves the Parsnip Patrol.

In 1991 Pat and I split up and I returned to Canada. What had I missed? In Vancouver, the Frances Street Squats were a row of six buildings squatted for nine months in 1990. Several of my friends had been involved, gaining alliances from their paying tenant neighbours through community-mindedness and activities. The Vancouver Police Department evicted the squatters eventually, in "Operation Overkill."[49] What else changed? Around about 1996 Chumbawamba signed with EMI; the corporation was no longer involved in arms manufacture. The band took this corporate money, wrote a blatantly anti-corporate record and "gave away their earnings to activities meant to hasten their benefactor's destruction."[50] The theatrical, punk-folk activists Chumbawamba, whose politics ran deep, hit the big time with *Tubthumping*.

---

49   *The Beat of Frances Street*, Eleven Foot Productions, December 1990. Available on YouTube in five parts, *http://www.youtube.com/watch?v=RZ1qSwo3kmE* (accessed July 24, 2014).

50   Aaron L. Smith, *Big Hands 5½: The Chumbawamba Issue* (zine, Cary, NC, December 2007).

I presumed street-cred whenever I trumpeted that I had loved them since the eighties.

I've been electronically scanning a few of those boxy little old pictures for Facebook, and a couple of ragged original *Cheeky Rebels*. It's time to put them all away and look outside at the rain again, how the wind moves it across the bay in columns. I should probably go out and tighten a few ropes.

Early in 2013 Joe Keithley, alias Joey Shithead, disbanded D.O.A. so that he could focus his energy on running for political office under a new set of initials: NDP for New Democratic Party. I suspect, however, that he will tour again. D.O.A. is in his DNA. I'm just grateful I got to interview him several years ago. At the band's last Tofino show I placed copies of their front-of-the-stage flyer on tables and in people's hands. Many young men scoffed or looked incredulous, even angry. This was good. It indicated that their store of experience was expanding to include a fresh viewpoint.

And the bands play on. Mecca Normal is busier than ever. Victoria's Nomeansno is still playing after more than thirty years, with their hook "Old is the New Young." There is still so much to sing about. In February 2013 an all-woman band, the Abbie Hoffman Society, were opening for Nomeansno in Nanaimo. I enjoyed their song "Trailer Park." The punk world I've been privileged to know does not lack humour. In an interview on CBC Radio's Brent Bambury show, *Day 6*, on April 13, 2013, Joe Keithley named the late Ronald Reagan "most responsible for the rise of punk rock in North America."[51] So that wasn't exclusively my experience after all!

I was drawn to the political consciousness, the freedom to express anger and demand justice; the ecstasy; the trust when leaping from

---

51   Brent Bambury, "Billy Bragg, Joey Keithley and Mike Watt on Political Music in the Thatcher Years," *Day 6* (CBC Radio, April 13, 2013), http://www.cbc.ca/day6/blog/2013/04/12/billy-bragg-joey-keithley-and-mike-watt-on-political-music-in-the-thatcher-years/ (accessed July 22, 2014).

a stage; the insistent questioning and remaking. The Tofino Legion's days of hosting SNFU, the Dayglos or the Real McKenzies may be over, and I may have to be content with listening to my iPod on the bike or in the boat as my "Halloween hair" blows around. But if anyone thinks it's not punk to live out in nature they should visit during a storm.

In memory of Dave Gregg, 1960–2014.

Haven Central

Though my grandmother and my uncles gardened in our backyard, I don't recall any communal gardens in North or central Vancouver when I was growing up. Yet in 1928, the City of Vancouver initiated a garden allotment program, and in 1943, allotments were among the fifty-two thousand Victory Gardens that were cultivated as part of the Lower Mainland's contribution to the war effort. There is one near my sister's home, not far from Lonsdale Quay, with a painted ceramic gate and benches. Both food and flowers grow there. I love to take a detour through it, or make it the highlight of a walk, whatever season. My nephew and I have seen a hummingbird there in November.

Although I don't need to use a communal garden myself, I'm glad they exist. I appreciate that they give people who may not have the space at home an opportunity to grow their own food. The shared garden offers a change of scenery, a chance to get out into the community. People can talk to neighbours they might otherwise only nod to, and some even become friends. If "agriculture has always been, and remains, a part of all cities"[52] as my old roommate Nedjo Rogers wrote in his master's thesis in 1990, the gardens are carrying on a noble tradition.

---

52   Nedjo Rogers, "Modern Commons: Place, Nature, and Revolution at the Strathcona Community Gardens" (master's thesis, Simon Fraser University, 1990).

These gardens not only get folks talking, they also enable the growing, eating and selling of healthy local food.[53] People start to think about what they eat and where it comes from. The huge carbon footprint we create by consuming food shipped from elsewhere shrinks drastically. Being active, creative and productive outdoors also improves mental and physical health. Gardeners learn from each other. There is fun even in failure. Some people use the tenets of permaculture in urban communal gardening: taking lessons from nature itself, modelling natural "gardens" to help define how we humans can live, using all manner of spaces (including roofs, walls and other vertical planes) to grow beautiful and edible plants.

Given that our way of life is no longer sustainable, this movement to gardening is encouraging. Those who grow food are ahead of the game. Food is energy, and growing it ourselves puts the power back into our own hands, giving us control over our diets, health and budgets and reclaiming power from corporations. Communal garden plots exemplify a way of learning, a means of empowering communities, and therapy too. As Nedjo noted, a garden can be called an education centre, a healing centre and a refuge for wildlife and humans. Garden plots can be the grocery store for people on low incomes, not a hobby but a necessity. Perhaps they may never own land, but with shared urban plots, they can grow food.

One of the scariest predictions I have heard is that to keep up with current human population growth, more food will have to be produced worldwide in the next fifty years than has been produced over the past ten thousand.[54] Moreover, we will have to produce this food

53   "Good Green News: Vancouver Urban Gardens," YouTube video, 3:24 (October 27, 2011), http://www.youtube.com/watch?v=dPD3BogYAKw (accessed July 23, 2014).

54   Ian Sample, "Global Food Crisis Looms as Climate Change and Population Growth Strip Fertile Land," the *Guardian*, August 31, 2007, http://www.theguardian.com/environment/2007/aug/31/climatechange.food (accessed July 22, 2014).

with less oil, water, farmland, climate stability and genetic diversity than we're accustomed to.

I began gardening in my mid-twenties, in awe of a woman named Bee I met on the Walbran Valley blockade. Bee knew everything about growing vegetables, healing with herbs and harvesting wild plants. She could do anything, and I felt daunted by her amazing competence, but I didn't let that stop me! Slugs, it turned out, were my biggest hurdle. Copper interferes with their slime, so I wound copper tape around our garden containers. Double width.

Later, the caretaker of Indian Island in Grice Bay allowed my partner and me to garden on his turf with three other locals. This was a special situation. The island is traditional Tla-o-qui-aht territory, inhabited at the time by Matt Sayachapis and his teenaged son, Ben. Matt and Ben had cleared thickets of thorny salmonberry for the garden plots and found midden soil: jackpot. Middens are any gardener's dream but in an ecosystem where soil is so thin whole forests must sprout from and live off their dead—known as nurse logs—it is closer to a miracle. Middens are former refuse sites for the Tla-o-qui-ahts; in them are generations' worth of the shells and bones from ocean-harvested meals. I used to joke that the seeds dropped from a quick lunch of tomato sandwiches would turn into plants by dinnertime. It wasn't far from the truth.

The Indian Island gardens enjoyed their own microclimate, trapping heat in the otherwise mild or moderate ecosystem that is Clayoquot Sound. The remaining salmonberry bushes attracted hummingbirds that would dive-bomb our heads, especially if we wore brightly coloured hats. We gardened there during one of the very few summers when grey whales took up residence in Grice Bay. To hear the blowhole exhalations of three huge whales as we worked was unforgettable.

A few years later, the floathouse "happened," triggering the idea to build a floating greenhouse. No whales ever come near this bay, but porpoises do. The greenhouse has proven its worth as a toilet for minks and river otters, an orgy for bees, even a playground for a marten, but mainly it's been my herb, flower and vegetable garden since 1998. There is nothing wrong with growing flowers in troubled times for honeybees.

My garden floats on a bay in the Sound, but I'd be growing the same things—possibly more—if I had a greenhouse on the ground in town where the air is a tad warmer overnight. Gardening and composting in Tofino requires a lookout for horsetail, salal, banana slugs and bears, as well as dandelions. A children's plot behind the elementary school managed by the Parent Advisory Council and the Raincoast Education Society allows the kids to grow food they can then cook or prepare in class. Roger Doiron, in his talk "My Subversive (Garden) Plot," calls gardening a "gateway drug" to other beneficial endeavours such as learning to cook and can/preserve.[55]

Eight community plots have been constructed at Tofino Botanical Gardens. Tofino lies on the end of a peninsula, most of which is a tsunami zone. In the event of a tsunami we would be cut off from virtually all our food supply. Our own gardens could be destroyed, but if they're not, they might be the only thing feeding us, the only thing saving us from total helplessness.

So, bread—and roses. The perennial appearance of flowers (edible or not) makes life so much sweeter. What is this human need for beauty? I wait impatiently every year for crocuses and salmonberry blooms, daffodils, ditches lighting up with yellow skunk cabbages; tulips, cherry blossoms, columbines and sweet william, white thimbleberry blooms, the Nootka rose and the great phallic flowers of horse chestnut trees. I sprinkle nasturtium and calendula petals in salads.

---

55   Roger Doiron, "My Subversive (Garden) Plot," TED video, 18:48 (September 2011), http://www.ted.com/talks/roger_doiron_my_subversive_garden_plot (accessed July 22, 2014). See also Kitchen Gardeners International (http://kgi.org), Doiron's non-profit community gardening association.

Bury my nose in the white honey-scented net of tiny alyssums. Whether I'm at home or in the city.

> All the little rain puddles
> shine yellow with pollen.
> Group the planters closely around the chair;
> pull the flowers near.
> Surround the chair with blooms.
> Sit bracketed by scent,
> by colour.
> Hemmed in by joy.
> Buffered by beauty.
> Protected by purity.
> Bees come close, rest on your body,
> offer no danger.
> When they tussle with the stamens
> next to your ear,
> a sudden powdering of pollen,
> baptism by bee.[56]

---

56   Christine Lowther, untitled. Previously unpublished.

THE WILD IN THE CITY,
THE CITY IN THE WILD

You have squandered us
turned our rummaging
into thievery.

—Sheila Peters,
"A Song for the Sorrow of Crows"

Skunks were unheard of on North Vancouver streets when I was grow-ing up. Now they strut around like they belong, or like they have nowhere else to go because the forest they used to live in has been cleared. This morning I'm up early enough to see a skunk on Lonsdale eating garbage.

Across the water, near Granville Street in the afternoon: a young gull, its tail to the sidewalk, one wing unfolded, facing the closed door of a boarded-up shop. I stop to look, it turns and our eyes meet: the wing folds, back to normal, perhaps not injured after all. Not wishing to scare it, I keep going. I have a bus to catch.

My bus comes. I get on, sit down, look back. The gull is walking slowly along the sidewalk in a land paved with perils. Looks nervous. *Can* it fly? Does it obey the red-handed "Wait" signal at the intersec-tion? People walk quickly past, as if the bird is invisible to them. I am whisked away. Everybody who isn't me has a fancy smartphone, but can anyone key a number for wildlife rescue? I don't ask.

Stanley Park: I head for Prospect Point. Kathy released our moth-er's ashes here many years ago. Three small young raccoons creep as closely as they dare to the nearest clump of humans. I am reminded of Russell Thornton's poem about a visit from three raccoons who paused at his sliding glass door and peered inside: "their three soft flames flaring through all my cells."[57] These three today seek handouts. Have been fed before. I think of the bear back in Tofino entering the tennis court. I think of the cougar at the Empress Hotel in Victoria. Both so unlike these little coons. So unlike the skunk or the gull. Yet all are wild animals, habituated by humans.

No longer fitting in either the pet or the wild camps, urban wild animals are now "pests." We have made it so. The tennis court bear was eventually shot—like so many others. "A fed bear is a dead bear." I love civilization, yet it can be poison to other beings. It can trap us in sleep, every bird call our slept-through alarm.

Thinking of this issue triggers the memory of Des Kennedy's book *Living Things We Love to Hate*, in which he educates and entertains the reader with facts and anecdotes on rats, bats, spiders, slugs, starlings and many other animals, as well as some invasive plants. Raccoons, too.

But I didn't hear about Toronto's baby raccoon killer until I read an article in Australia's *Animal Studies Journal* out of the University of Wollongong, "Tales of Cruelty and Belonging: In Search of an Ethic for Urban Human-Wildlife Relations" by Erin Luther. In 2011, a man was charged with cruelty to animals and possessing a dangerous weapon for attacking baby raccoons with a shovel in his backyard. A neighbour heard the babies screaming, saw what was happening and called the police. The mother raccoon hovered nearby, trying to get to her babies. One of the injured was retrieved by police. The attacker became an instant media celebrity, spawning public debates ranging between demands for stricter laws against cruelty to cries for lethal control of urban raccoons. There was even a demonstration where both anti- and pro-raccoon protesters rallied. As Luther points out, the animals that

---

57   "they presented proof of what could not be made into lies, they brought out into the open what was circling within my sight ..." Russell Thornton, "Raccoons," *The Human Shore* (Madeira Park, BC: Harbour Publishing, 2006).

share our urban spaces with us, but not as pets, become liminal to us. Do they, or do they not, belong in the city? Not having a clear answer strikes fear into us. "Raccoons—irreverent, indecent transgressors of the boundaries that separate us from our own animality—threaten the boundaries of the urban moral order."[58]

When I'm squashing the life out of aphids or voracious caterpillars in my garden I wonder if I've brought this urban moral order with me to my uncivilized bay. Or when I'm planning to bring in an exterminator to deal with a hornets' nest growing inside the walls of my floathouse. Or stomping on ants. Or when I resent the sweetest, most graceful pair of swallows for building a seaweed nest on an overhang right outside my door, for chasing away the hummingbirds and pooping everywhere.

Years ago I wrote a poem about waking to the horror of a flailing wolf spider in my water glass, about refusing to watch *The Nature of Things* because of the kills (lion on wildebeest); about dragonflies eating helpless bugs alive, their prey's discarded wings falling down from the feast. The Toronto man with the shovel? He was not killing to survive, but for convenience. His only defence? Rage. We want animals to be nice. We want them unbothersome, or not at all: according to Gavan Watson, we want them "meek, unusual, melodious, and accessible on our terms."[59]

Since I wrote this, a raccoon has come in through the cats' flap during the night. Dangerous, messy, inconvenient. Defensive strategy required. A war begun.

A post about a new book from the University of Minnesota Press,

---

58   Erin Luther, "Tales of Cruelty and Belonging: In Search of an Ethic for Urban Human-Wildlife Relations," *Animal Studies Journal* 2, no. 1 (2013): 35–54.

59   Gavan P.L. Watson, "See Gull: Cultural Blind Spots and the Disappearance of the Ring-Billed Gull in Toronto," in *Trash Animals: How We Live with Nature's Filthy, Feral, Invasive, and Unwanted Species*, ed. Kelsi Nagy and Phillip David Johnson II (Minneapolis: University of Minnesota Press, 2013).

Trash Animals: How We Live with Nature's Filthy, Feral, Invasive, and Unwanted Species, appeared on a blog by *Orion* magazine.[60] Here are two responses:

> Whatever is abundant in any given area (even if it's rare and valued in another), qualifies to be eradicated because of its inherent presence, as if it dares to co-exist in our fabricated realm with us. Even more so if it dares to display any evidence of the same functions as humans (noise, waste, building shelter, courtship, protecting young ones). In a way, I think we project our own self-hatred and disgust onto animals much in the same way we project other emotions, rather than simply appreciating them for their own.[61]

> My view of "trash" animals is that they have managed to adapt to human environments, which are usually dirty and contaminated. But humans, as arrogant as we are, attribute our filth on to the other animals who had nothing to do with it. "Roaches are disgusting!" we'll say—yes, but mostly because they live in human filth, not their own.[62]

However I feel about "inconvenient" wildlife at any given moment, one of the things I love most about cities is the wildlife I glimpse there.

60   Scott Gast, "On Packrat Philosophy, Cantankerous Grasshoppers, and Living with Nature's Unwanted Species," the *Orion* Blog, June 19, 2013, http://www.orionmagazine.org/index.php/newsfrom187/entry/7580/ (accessed July 23, 2014).
61   Caral Dawn, blog comment on "On Packrat Philosophy, Cantankerous Grasshoppers, and Living with Nature's Unwanted Species."
62   Eric, blog comment on "On Packrat Philosophy, Cantankerous Grasshoppers, and Living with Nature's Unwanted Species."

Skunks included. Gulls are not so mysterious to me, thanks to their ubiquity and everydayness—and what Gavan Watson calls "cultural blindness."[63] I did not know what species of gull stood at that downtown door. Stranger than that was the sense of my being the only one seeing it at all.

Now that the swallows' chicks outside my door have hatched, there are five fluffy, hungry, pooping babies to think about. I have moved the hummingbird feeders and changed a few other things around. What I thought was bothersome has shifted: now when there's a kingfisher that comes too close, I leap up and get ready to chase it off. (The parents might be busy chasing off a raven.) Still, what a lot of poop. And when they start pushing each other out of the nest, what then: adoption? I imagine a lot of work. I am owned by birds. I must duck to avoid protective barn swallows out my back door, have to dodge jostling hummers out my front door. Oh well, it's not like they're pigeons ...

---

63   Gavan Watson, "See Gull: Cultural Blind Spots and the Disappearance of the Ring-billed Gull in Toronto," in *Trash Animals*, ed. Kelsi Nagy and Phillip David Johnson.

GIBSON STREET FIREWEED

In Tofino there's one section of road that remains unpaved. And while I hope it stays that way (and I've sent many letters to council begging them to leave it be), I know it may soon don the conformist uniform of pavement and streetlights. For now, though, it is one of the few places in town still good for stargazing.

In summer daylight hours—before the visit of the Olympic flame called for re-gravelling and widening—dragonflies would lazily hover and dart back and forth across Gibson between the elementary school and the child care centre. You might have noticed, as I did, fireweed blooming alongside the road. You might have spotted the one plant broken or cut along its main stem. As a result of the early injury, instead of growing straight and tall with its deep pink flowers concentrated at the top, it branched out and flowered more profusely than all the unbroken ones. Every branch aflame. The blooms may not have been focussed but they were everywhere, crooked and sweet. A dazzling compensation.

PART 3
MERGE

Guerilla Scribbler

The child is making nonsense again, wasting time when she could be playing, but at least it's her own time and not her parents'. And it keeps her quiet—busy, almost studious—and she's smiling instead of whining or complaining. Silly thing fancying herself industrious, clever, or good. She has what must be her older sister's workbook from school open and laid flat, the blank lines waiting for answers to questions. She learned to read at age three, a year ago now. But she still can't write, or rather, print. Yet there she sits, scribbling onto the lines, believing—feeling passionately—that she's writing. How does this inane activity keep her fulfilled? She can go for half an hour at a time, or until her sister distracts her. She has almost filled the notebook.

In a couple of years the child will be writing novels—ten chapters, illustrated. *The Adventures of Bobby and his Grandmother. The Deer of the Wind.* A romantic from the beginning. Her father will print *Deer* in his self-published magazine, *Pegasus.* Complete with her drawings.

The child turns around to find herself without parents, with police, on a boat with her equally silent sister. She turns again and faces an infuriating boy in the foster home, who chases her all over the house, oblivious to her shameful losses. She retreats into *Charlotte's Web*, oak trees and a green declension out back that she rolls down. Never again to be touched by either parent, the child knows she's still alive when solid ground embraces her.

The next foster home is hosted by religious fanatics. She can't write.

The revolving door leads to her mother's mother. Gramma is old and has heart disease. The child remains disturbed, abrasive. It's a recipe for Ordeal in a ten-year package. How do either of them survive those years? How does her sister, who continues in the foster home circuit? Revolution, every year. Turning and turning.

Like when the child turns thirteen and decides to try a group home. Presto! instant family: four new sisters. Makeup, curling irons, tight jeans, boys, smoking, toking. She writes of nothing but suicidal despair, a new low for adolescent literary accomplishment. After eleven months she flees back to Gram's and throws away the dog-eared notebook of desperate ruminations.

As high school progresses, she narrowly escapes expulsion; then a creative writing course is offered in eleventh grade. Inner revolution of the life-saving kind.

I write on buses and at bus stops. I write at a friend's house with our cups of tea. I write and it's rude. I write when I'm alone on Granville Street, watching birds fly between skyscrapers. It doesn't matter that she doesn't know others have done so before her.

I am an angel. My wings are my hands, and the fingers do not function without a pen. Talk about teenage declaration. It's in the genes. She moves to claim her birthright.

She can see for miles in every direction, and can smell the low tide far below; she kicks off her sandals, hurls them toward the ruined castle doorway—this is a moment that imprints itself forever—she throws up her arms and flies down the sandy cliff. Her goal is the cave and the stone circle, but it's the flight, that short ecstatic journey, that still feeds.

It's bloody lucky at nineteen years old to be in such a sympathetic landscape, so far from her origins. Turning outward to adventure is sweet relief; turning inward can come later. Exploring, letter-writing, journaling. Attempting love.

Five years on, she can hear the blackbird singing, can touch the cow parsley thick along the roadsides, can get a whiff of manure on the fields, and knows this place and time is sweetest now that she will be leaving. The cuckoo calls.

The child has other learning to do: how to heal, how to garden, how to get along, how to break up, how to cope. The scribbling never stops. Suitcases stuffed full of diaries. Habit, not discipline. Need, not practice. Words and more words. A wise writer points out that, sooner or later, rather than sitting in class, scribblers need to shut themselves away alone and write.

The last place to imagine, the last place to write from, the last place to heal, the long-ago wordless interior of a police boat.

PHOTO KATE PAUL CRAIG.

WE TREMBLE IN RESPONSE: FAMISHED FOR GRIEF

⤳

We have lived in a catastrophic time. The redundancy of violence and suffering, the sheer immensity of the danger, always threatens to wither the imagination, to make us turn back to the purely personal, as if it were somehow more real because the mind can, at least, compass it, whereas the effort to think about the fate of the planet ... comes to us mostly as dark and private musings.

—Robert Hass, introduction to
Robinson Jeffers's Rock and Hawk

We need to cultivate as many resources as possible if we are going to address our planet's challenges. These resources aren't just external. They are also internal. They are capacities we can build; in the same way we have built our collective intelligence and our capacity for reason.

—Jeff Warren, "Environmentalism and the Mind,"
Psychology Tomorrow

How did Beth and I, at four and five, grieve for the two old trees in south Vancouver that we had tried to save with our homemade placards and our mother? How did our mother cope with her own disappointment, anger and sorrow? I know she had to break the bad news to us, yet I have no memory of the aftermath.

In April 1982, I sat alone on a Vancouver bus heading to my first peace march. A wavy-haired boy smiled at me from his seat. We disembarked together and began talking on our way to the event. Our friendship has continued to this day. Such is the openness of teenagers; Kevin was fifteen, I was fourteen. The joy of walking for peace encouraged me to become more involved in the anti-nuclear movement, even bringing my convictions to school with me.

For weeks I carried a petition to every class, gathering signatures behind teachers' backs against American cruise missile testing in Canadian skies. I watched the looks on my peers' faces as they took in facts and statistics uncovered by End the Arms Race (EAR). Hundreds of kids signed, yet the only result was a letter from our MP patting me on the head saying, *Don't worry, I know better than you and this testing is a good thing.* Only the guidance systems and not the warheads were being tested.

"Oh," I thought. "That's all right then! Canada can keep its reputation as a peace-loving nation. As if."

Simply by being alive and awake in the 1980s, my classmates and I learned of horrors no teenager should ever have to consider. The warhead on every cruise missile was about seven and a half times as powerful as one atom bomb. Operation Dismantle told us that enough nukes were stockpiled around the world to destroy the human race at least twenty times. Just after my sixteenth birthday, *The Day After* was shown on TV. More than one hundred million people saw America depicted in graphic detail as a blackened wasteland of burned-out cities filled with burn, blast and radiation victims in the resultant nuclear winter.[64] How did we cope? It would be at least another year before I discovered the balm of punk music, started producing *Cheeky Rebel* and writing things like this:

> Does anybody care about this planet? This is the only place where life exists. Yet people don't realize that the only real world in the universe is jeopardizing itself to complete obliteration. The old days where whole cities or even countries were in danger are over; no longer are we talking of the USA and the USSR. One bomb and the planet … So if you're still in the dark abyss of ignorance, quit chanting the blind words, "better dead than red," 'cause there won't be the slightest chance in hell for turning red—or black, or yellow, or brown, or purple—in the case of WW 3. You won't be around to fight for democracy.

When my grade twelve history teacher lectured that the 1945 atomic bombings of Hiroshima and Nagasaki were justified, I quoted Dr. Helen Caldicott to him. My friend Marielle and I had practically memorized Caldicott's documentary *If You Love This Planet*. During a film that glorified war weaponry (shown by the same teacher), I walked out of class. Little did I know that in a couple of years' time, I'd be travelling to the tense, bombed-out city of Belfast and living under Thatcher.

In the meantime the wholesome beauty of North Vancouver, particularly Lynn Canyon, offered an escape of sorts. Although the canyon was a party spot for some, I mostly just walked there on weekends to enjoy the forest and the river. But any place could potentially be

---

64   *The Day After*, directed by Nicholas Meyer (ABC Circle Films, 1983).

wiped out by a single nuclear accident, whether from cruise missiles overhead or nuke-carrying American warships in the harbour. On August 6, 1985, the fortieth anniversary of Hiroshima, EAR organized an event where volunteers, my sister and me included, traversed the streets of Vancouver all night. While the city slept, we spray-painted human body outlines all over sidewalks. As Beth and I, bleary-eyed, fell upon a fast-food breakfast, Vancouver's population woke to eerie shadow imprints just like the ones left in Hiroshima forty years previously. The markings were all that remained of tens of thousands of Japanese people vapourized by the two bombs. (Another thing I had to learn outside of high school was how Canadians of Japanese descent were rounded up after the attack on Pearl Harbor, their homes and belongings confiscated, families and friends separated and sent to internment camps away from the coast.)

> Pain for the world is normal, healthy, and widespread.
>
> —Joanna Macy,
> *Active Hope: How to Face the Mess We're in without Going Crazy*[65]

College was next, where I took Sociology 210—Current Social Issues: War and Peace, a class on the nuclear arms race, taught by a peace activist. And my nightmares began: I dreamed Vancouver's downtown night lights, visible from my North Van bedroom window, were extinguished by a sickening blast almost beyond normal senses, felt beneath the skin. Just a few of the course's goals of study:

- the psychosocial impact of nuclearism in our time
- the student's awareness of the nuclear age and its grave threat to the continuation of society and humanity

---

65   Joanna Macy and Chris Johnstone, *Active Hope: How to Face the Mess We're in without Going Crazy* (Novato, CA: New World Library, 2012).

- assessing the likelihood of an accidental nuclear war
- and [this is where I insert a smiley face] providing a positive framework for understanding what role we can play in bringing about changes to the nuclear threat.

During the day I would break into a clammy sweat sitting in class—any class—and every meeting, looking out the window for a mushroom cloud. How could people act so normally while someone's finger was poised over the button of annihilation?

> World war—lotsa fun—people in a panic on the run
> White House is aimin' the gun—people in a panic on the run
> The Kremlin's aimin' the gun
> We're pawns in the middle
> Sitting ducks with no acquittal …
>
> I don't really wanna die! World War Three
> With A-bombs dropping from the sky! World War Three
> Don't give me your reasons why! World War Three
> Just know I don't wanna die.
>
> —D.O.A., "World War Three"[66]

Phrases looped repetitively in my ears: "just and unjust wars," "logic of exterminism," "Star Wars." Soc 210 should have come with mandatory counselling, or at the very least Joanna Macy's *Despair and Personal Power in the Nuclear Age* on its reading list. I dropped the course. Never made it as far as the "positive framework." For once, journaling was not helping my state of mind.

---

66   D.O.A., "World War Three" (Joe Keithley/Chuck Biscuits, Prisoner Publishing, SOCAN).

Maybe I have no guts
Maybe I love you all too much
But I can't sleep I can't breathe
It's tearing me up, it's tearing me up
It's tearing the heart out of me

—Nomeansno, "One Fine Day"[67]

A short year later, in 1987, I travelled to Belfast and joined a volunteer group for children of both Protestant and Catholic backgrounds. Teens and preteens, probably the children's older siblings, wandered abandoned, ruined neighbourhoods in gangs and threw bottles at us. We spent time with each sect of younger kids, then tried to bring them together at a new playground. The children tore the playground down; we didn't or couldn't stop them. It was fun for them. Maybe they were bringing down the system, in their own way. Maybe they were in cathartic release, getting that system out of their system.

Another year later, in England, I began an introductory course in re-evaluation counselling (RC). How to explain RC, also called co-counselling? RC is based on deep, nonjudging listening between laypersons—it can tackle everything from personal disappointments and grief to racism, sexism, homophobia and environmental angst. Such a practice might have been the only way of remaining in the dreaded Soc 210. Come to think of it, RC would be a boon to any first-year college student, in any program! I applied it mostly to personal relationships and my past.

England's animal rights movement was also claiming much of my attention. While learning a lot from yearly Cruelty-Free Fayres in London, I still fled from documentaries about the horrors of animal

---

67   Nomeansno, "One Fine Day," lyrics written by Robert Wright, copyright Wrong Records.

use and abuse: fox hunting, hare coursing, badger baiting, live cosmetics testing, dairy production, mink farms, live exports and so on, ad infinitum. Much easier to go out and fuck directly with such time-honoured traditions: namely, by joining the Hunt Saboteurs Association and participating in protests, stickering cosmetics in stores, picketing farms. The Parsnip Patrol organized a benefit concert for Sea Shepherd, the folks who use direct action to stop whaling all over the world. Ativistic and Epidemic played Whitstable Labour Club, as did Mecca Normal from Vancouver.

In 1991 I went back to Canada. The Soviet Union collapsed, signalling an end to the Cold War. For better or for worse, nuclear Armageddon was already much diminished in my mind. That summer and the next, activists blocked clearcut logging in the Walbran Valley and in Clayoquot Sound. By 1993, hundreds of people were joining the blockades. Beth risked arrest on August 9, the peak day of three hundred arrests, and her birthday.

I was an early-morning eco-office person that summer, not brave enough to live at the blockade's base camp, which was in a vast, burned clearcut named the Black Hole. "Peacekeeping" was employed to calm irate loggers, and "burnout" (psychological and emotional exhaustion) was simply one more agenda item in lengthy meetings with many other urgent items demanding time and energy. I was fortunate to meet fellow activist Susan Kammerzell. She happened to be skilled in RC. My class in England had been interrupted by travel, so I was glad to refresh with Susan. She has remained one of my dearest friends to this day. Quite recently I happened to read the following quotation and felt her presence as strongly as if she were sitting beside me again:

> There are those ... who are not frightened of grief;
> dropping deep into the sorrow, they find therein a nec-
> essary elixir to the numbness ... Grief is but a gate,

and our tears a kind of key opening a place of wonder that's been locked away. Suddenly we notice the sustaining resonance between the drumming heart within our chest and the pulse rising from under the ground.

—David Abram, *Becoming Animal*[68]

Susan once wrote in an essay:

> When I learned how to better listen to people, they told me more: we are famished for opportunities to safely grieve environmental damage … We are sturdy and skilled enough to survive the grieving and grow … Creating opportunities to mourn effectively is deeply beneficial to environmental work, and to living here on Earth.[69]

Unfortunately, Susan and I settled far apart. Nobody else I knew was into RC. New realities like the hole in Earth's ozone layer, greenhouse gases, plastic in Earth's oceans, industrial fish farms, the Alberta tar sands and pipelines were worse than any nightmare. It was time to deal with the erosion of what had always been my strongest consolation: nature itself. Nature's doom was no war, no accident waiting to happen; it was the overall effect of business as usual, well under way. How to bear having to grieve for that which had always been my deepest, indeed my only healer?

A log cabin on a small, forested island in Clayoquot Sound in the mid-1990s proved a place for healing as well as creative expression and activism. I was lucky to have an incredibly supportive partner

---

68   David Abram, *Becoming Animal: An Earthly Cosmology* (New York/Toronto: Vintage Books and Random House, 2011).
69   Susan Kammerzell, untitled. Previously unpublished.

at the time. Still easily wounded, if I had to travel through too many miles of clearcuts I'd break down in hysterics. Being in that kind of logged-out landscape was like traversing the moon, or worse, a planet that used to be alive until humans butchered it. Like the time we were looking for access to the Clayoquot River Valley so that I could record early-morning signs of the threatened seabird, marbled murrelet. After many miles Warren had to stop the car because I was clinging to him, bawling into his neck. He completely understood.

Reading poetry proved an immediate support. Poets feel deeply and take deep action. *Witness to Wilderness*, a Clayoquot Sound anthology of poems, essays and photos published in 1994, gives expression to Canadians who care about public forests under threat. A modern example is Christine Leclerc's anthology *The Enpipe Line: 70,000+ Kilometres of Poetry Written in Resistance to the Enbridge Northern Gateway Pipelines Proposal*. From that collection:

> in my sleep i dreamed a poem
> that caused the despairing to shout for joy
> to embrace each other and weep tears of gladness
> in my sleep i dreamed a poem
> that healed the hurts of the earth and grew back the trees
> —Ivan Antoniw, "In My Sleep"[70]

There have always been political poets but the poetry that moves me most is often labelled "nature poetry." In essence, nature poems are activist poems because they trigger our love for our planet and inspire us to act for its protection. BC poet Susan McCaslin posted tree poems on the trees of an endangered wood. Catherine Owen's *The Wrecks of Eden* mourns extinct species:

---

70 Ivan Antoniw, "In My Sleep," in *The Enpipe Line: 70,000+ Kilometres of Poetry Written in Resistance to the Enbridge Northern Gateway Pipelines Proposal* (Smithers, BC: Creekstone Press, 2012).

What path did they take through the woods
and in what last den lie down?
                    —"Where did they go?"[71]

As for the poetry in song, sometimes I can't bear listening to Bruce
Cockburn's song "Beautiful Creatures," which grieves for species disappearing now:

> Like a dam on a river
> my conscience is pressed
> by the weight of hard feelings
> piled up in my breast
> the callous and vicious things
> humans display
> the beautiful creatures are going away[72]

Singer-songwriters like Dana Lyons, with his album *Turn of the
Wrench*, are vessels for the voice of planet Earth. Hearing Dana for the
first time was just as reaffirming for me as finding punk had been,
because we were living on the blockades, taking direct action for the
planet's forests, and his lyrics belonged to the setting:

> And in my heart, the chains falling apart
> the wildness in my soul
> and for once in life, for once in life I know
> I'm not alone, for the mountains make our bones
> with the oceans in our blood
> our feet planted, planted firmly in the mud

71   Catherine Owen, *The Wrecks of Eden* (Hamilton, ON: Wolsak & Wynn, 2001).
72   Bruce Cockburn, "Beautiful Creatures," lyrics written by Bruce Cockburn (SOCAN), copyright Rotten
Kiddies Music LLC (BMI).

we are alive, the burning embers in our eyes
the tingling touch upon our skin
and in the heat of passion we begin to understand
that we are of this land
that we are part of Earth
and when it's threatened, we will fight for all we're worth ...[73]

As a child I looked to beetles for answers in my own private citadel of leaves, sought solace in thickets; I traded classrooms for shrubberies, notebooks for leaves and grass, lessons for Narnia in the crowns of walnut trees, friends for insects mute and miraculous. Nowadays I'm full of emoting or "discharging" for the village I live in, its small green ruralities disappearing under pavement. "Now the machines have moved in / cut their swath, cast kinks / of intestine and bowel, / spewed tree sap and bush blood. / Our feet keep to the centre of the new path / and suffer the truth: we tread / through someone's remains, / stand in their guts, tempt Devil's Snare."[74] I have had to shrug off embarrassment about composing poems with crying and blubbing in them. In a poem about Gibson Street, I confess to copious weeping for the broken fireweed plant that now blooms all the more profusely and riotously. I cry for a creek that somehow, during a rainforest's very first drought, never dries up completely. I compose a dirge for the disappearance of bees and beg to know how a forest loses its rain and where its bees disappear to. Of course, there are other valid ways to "discharge," like laughing, shouting, yawning and shaking. When facing pain or joy, "we tremble in response, a stirring of branches, / ripples on water, / a frisson of déjà vu."[75]

---

73 Dana Lyons, "Drop of Water," copyright 1996 Lyons Brothers Music BMI, used with permission. http://www.cowswithguns.com

74 Christine Lowther, "Forbidden Forest" in *Half-Blood Poems: Inspired by the Stories of J.K. Rowling* (Hamden, CT: Zossima Press, 2011).

75 Christine Lowther, "Green Man." Previously unpublished.

A few years ago at a punk rock film festival in Victoria, I saw footage of a live pig being butchered as it hung from a hook and a monkey suffering through vivisection. It was not until I wrote these witnessings into a poem that I could bear feeling what I had seen. When I heard on the news that hundreds of pieces of plastic were found inside a single seabird's stomach, I felt paralyzed and numb until I wrote. In April 2010, when the oil drilling rig exploded in the Gulf of Mexico, I floundered in fear until working through it in words. It helped even more when a member of my writers' group suggested I write from the point of view of the spilled plume:

> A planet's blood belongs buried,
> embedded in rock,
> soothing friction between fossils.
> You think I wanted release
> into this fluidic expanse?
> I'd as soon spout off into Space.
> Yet here I find myself,
> with the heaviness gone;
> there is light. I am light.[76]

In her 2012 book *Active Hope: How to Face the Mess We're in without Going Crazy*, Joanna Macy writes, "If you're feeling sickened by a disturbing news report, you can step into gratitude simply by focussing on your breath and taking a moment to give thanks for whatever may be sustaining you in that moment."[77] It is wonderful that in reading we are solitary yet not alone. For me—whether I'm sustained in that reeling, breathing moment by direct action, Skype-style RC with Susan or poetry—it's about reaching out. There is a spacious, freeing relief and

---

76   Christine Lowther, "In Conversation." Previously unpublished.
77   Joanna Macy and Chris Johnstone, *Active Hope.*

release in sharing environmental concern and grief. Alone and inactive, we can feel helpless, traumatized, shrunken and powerless.

> Now if you
> cringe and shrink inside
> but say nothing
> nothing to no one
>
> …
>
> forget your life
> it's nothing

—Nomeansno, "Forget Your Life"[78]

Coming together with fellow beings also heals the ambivalence some of us feel toward our own species: I don't want to see humanity as a cancer. Dislodging my sorrow renews hope and strengthens resolve. It is up to each individual to decide what form one's sharing will take. For me at first it was the activism itself that was the sharing: a joining up, an entering into communities of concern and action. When the activism became overwhelming, I limited my exposure to the disturbing information while still participating. Later came the co-counselling. Most recently poetry has been my saviour. When I set out to write this essay I thought it was just those three, but I now realize that music (and not just punk) is also a source of creativity, community and a sharing to lean on. As Lorri Neilsen Glenn writes in *Threading Light: Explorations in Loss and Poetry*: "Art grounds our grief in form; it connects us to one another and to the world."[79]

---

78 Nomeansno, "Forget Your Life," lyrics written by Robert Wright, copyright Wrong Records.
79 Lorri Neilsen Glenn, *Threading Light: Explorations in Loss and Poetry* (Regina, SK: Hagios Press, 2011).

And though I may falter, and though I may stumble
and though I may weave, and though I may fall
I will stand up, I'll beat the odds
'cos I'm gonna get there, even if I have to crawl

—D.O.A., "I Make This World"[80]

MARIA, ME, MARIELLE, MORNA. PHOTO TINA NORVELL.

---

80   D.O.A., "I Make This World" (Joe Keithley, Prisoner Publishing, SOCAN).

A Beautiful Imposition

Here nature dwarfs the human. The environment is alternately
a place that overwhelms and destroys people, a place of refuge,
and a place of revelation. The space and grandeur of this place
decentres humans and so requires a rethinking of the meaning of
the human person.

—Patricia O'Connell Killen,
"Memory, Novelty and Possibility in This Place"

There are things I dislike about Tofino. Visitors and residents alike
think it's better than the city, but we have no fudge shop. No music
store. Not even one nightclub. No optometrist, no surgeons; no MRI
or CT scanners, no births in the little hospital; no lasting tattoo par-
lour. No meditation centre; too much yoga. No art supply store.

Something I do like is how artists take up challenges and find in-
novative ways to create. Many thrive on the one-hundred-mile diet,
setting a bioregional example: carvers and sculptors of wood—be it
salvaged, burls or driftwood. Others make baskets and jewellery from
kelp and beach glass. Quite a few of us write.

When author Sharon Butala came to Tofino, taught a workshop
and expressed belief in my ability as a prose writer, I felt a deep, re-
solved exhalation. It appeared I would not be letting go of the literary
grindstone. Before continuing, though, I have to face up to the healing
yet to be done. Poetry was how I healed my youth, and nature was the
conveyor of the poetry. Together, nature and poem writing conspired

to heal me, like an art therapy. Living in a wild place—where every leaf is its own poem—brings healing process and poetry together.

Poetry, says Marilyn Bowering, "takes us out of the chaos, lets us stand back and understand even while we are deeply involved in the process of living terrible contradictions."[81] I think of this in everyday moments. Smiling back at acquaintances in the post office, answering "I'm fine, thank you," in truth I sometimes feel poison behind these upturned lips because I'm not fine, not really. Poetic expression, for me, continues to equal repair, restoration and growth. Despite violent origins—the big bang, or an exploding apart of family—evolution occurs. Despite, or because of it, as Cormac McCarthy said, "Creative work is often driven by pain. It may be that if you don't have something in the back of your head driving you nuts, you may not do anything. It's not a good arrangement. If I were God, I wouldn't have done it that way."[82]

⌁

The mystery of the natural world lies in its power to evoke a human response, and in the variety of the potential responses.

—Fred Kaplan[83]

For ten years after the birth of my first poetry book, I kept mainly to non-fiction, pooh-poohing anyone who introduced me as a poet. The poems had dried up. Yet reading poetry eventually renewed my fascination with it. In time, while living close to Schooner Cove in Pacific Rim National Park, poems sprouted inside me, seeded

81   Marilyn Bowering, in her introduction to "Colour Theory," in *Rocksalt*, ed. Mona Fertig and Harold Rhenisch (Salt Spring Island, BC: Mother Tongue Publishing, 2008).

82   Cormac McCarthy, interviewed by John Jurgensen, "Hollywood's Favorite Cowboy," the *Wall Street Journal*, November 20, 2009, http://online.wsj.com/article/SB100014240527487045762045745297035772745 72.html (accessed July 24, 2014).

83   Fred Kaplan, *Lincoln: The Biography of a Writer* (Harper, 2008), quoted in *Sky* magazine, February 2009, page 88.

there by the outdoors. (Admittedly, it helped that I had just been dumped.) I was suddenly living the miraculous: writing a new poem every day.

My method of practice is, as my teenaged nephew likes to say, "random." I go for walks or bike rides in nature to find inspiration, as the splintering rain, gale-blown trees and reaching, crashing waves reflect how I feel.

This season

is all about motion, begs response from us,
wails against polite sunset-viewing. Caught
between roiling ocean, statues of shore rock
and standing stick-humans, no wonder

the self bleeds out my eyes.[84]

A place is land, and land is geology. Susan Musgrave wrote twenty meditations on stones. My mother was "madly in love" with stone, writing books called *Milk Stone* and *A Stone Diary*. Sharon Butala wrote *Wild Stone Heart*. In the Tofino area an island of rock at the end of a tombolo on Chesterman Beach is a favourite place, even a magical place for many. This is an excerpt from a poem I wrote during a productive autumn:

They say the place is a ley-line intersection:
peak of planetary pressure points,
the lure behind every Pacific coast pilgrimage.
There I've witnessed the wretched

---

84   Christine Lowther, "Full of Mad," in *My Nature*.

as they cried and clung to veined stone.
I've seen them kissing and caressing jagged rock.
Whether returning on dry sand or wading through
incoming tide,
their faces come down the tombolo blazing with new-
found peace.[85]

Rock, stone, bedrock—this is the foundation of place, as are the less stable surfaces of soft sand, extreme tides and miles of boot-sucking mudflats. Clayoquot Sound is a coastal place of plenty. Oystercatchers and marbled murrelets, unlogged mountains, oyster farms, solid weeks of rain, waterspouts, seals, whales, shaggy thousand-year-old cedars, boats and surfboards and kayaks. Then there's the Tuff Session Ale on karaoke night and stumbling to a party at Tonquin Beach without a flashlight ... there is almost too much to write about.

For me, writing about nature demands constant vigilance against sentimentality; the poet must blast any hint of a cliché off the page. Ruthless, driven and excitable describes me in this process, like the weather, like the environment. If I were walking in a pastoral setting rather than on a windy, wild beach fringed with grizzled forest, would my poems be softer? I hope not.

Winter is essential for catching up to dreams and goals. It means grounded, undistracted hours of writing and pitching, rewriting and editing. It allows a pyjama-clad holing up with projects. And when the storms cause power outages, I take walks and bicycle rides in search of my muse. Even a winter storm on my coast is comparatively mild. When the rest of Canada is buried under deep snow, men on Tofino's beaches—barefoot and shirtless—throw frisbees. The wild-yet-mild polarity can be a boon to the artful mind.

---

85   Christine Lowther, "Outcrop Island," in *My Nature*.

[T]he natural world is an inexhaustible source of meaning, directly available to us if we allow our contemplative attention to rest there ...

—Jan Zwicky[86]

Nature may be supportive, but where is the human scaffold for the creatively inclined out here? Where the stimulation? In a fudgeless locale, where can I turn? To books, writers' groups, reading clubs, visiting authors, the theatre society, disc jockeys and live bands. We even boast a highly organized Pacific Rim Arts Society. Still, a writer is always isolated. Sometimes the group doesn't meet for a long while. My own struggle has to do with juggling three day-jobs with alone time, my time for creating. Having enough energy to focus, to find the acutely awake state required for poem making, the uninterrupted hours required for prose writing. Busy season in a tourist town allows precious little of this writer's most coveted tool. When time presents itself at last, my energy is often too drained to make use of it.

Fortunately, I have mates who help me see through and break down the barriers I throw in my own way. My friend Anita reminded me recently that the idea that writers and artists *suffer* is far from stereotyping. She gave me a crucial affirmation. Suddenly, I am not a sour, resentful curmudgeon curtailed by writer's block. I am an artist! A long-suffering artist!

I have a 1950s photograph of eleven women and two children. My late poet-mother is one of the women. Unlike any of the others, she looks uncomfortable. I always wondered if she was in a lousy mood at the time of the photo, or whether she didn't like the photographer. Maybe she was miffed at her mum, who sits beside her, grinning widely.

---

86 Jan Zwicky, "Lyric Realism: Nature Poetry, Silence, and Ontology," *Malahat Review*, Winter 2008.

MY MOTHER IS SEATED ON THE FAR LEFT. SHE IS HOLDING MY BROTHER, ALAN. MY GRANDMOTHER IS BESIDE HER, AND THE OTHER CHILD IN THE PIICTURE IS MY SISTER KATHY.

One day the filmmaker Anne Henderson was studying this picture in her preparation for the documentary *Water Marks*.

"Look at her face," Anne said. "She knows she doesn't fit in. See? She was an *artist*."

True, someone else might interpret the expression differently. They might say, "She was a feminist." Her sister, my aunt, who is also in the picture, might explain, "She was exhausted and had one of her migraines coming on." Perhaps the pain in my mother's face is there because she wishes she could be happy and content with her lot, as the other women seem to be. The two children are my elder brother and sister. Today, I can't help but wonder if, in an era of traditional gender roles, she was longing for time and energy to write, and for acceptance of such yearning.

Mine is a different era with new freedoms and new constraints. Yet I envy the hell out of those who don't call themselves artists or writers. They are the free ones. Work, play, family, friends. Can't I be grateful for all I have? Oh, no. I have to write. A normal life could never be enough. *I* am never enough. I require the support of my fellow writers along with ample outings to forest, beach and mudflat.

⟫⟫

In my experience, west coast places *cause* art. Their beauty imposes itself upon our consciousness, and that imposition necessitates response. Poet Greg Simison says, for British Columbia poets, a poetry *of place* "is impossible for most of us to ignore when we live where the geography is so dominant."[87]

I wonder, too, does all this beauty invite open-mindedness and experimentation? Does the mild climate lower fears and soften conservatism? (We may have a right-wing government in British Columbia but not compared to Alberta, not compared to vast numbers of states south of the border.) What is it about our coast that gives birth to the bush dwellers living off-grid and making crafts to sell at Gulf Island weekend markets? For answers, we could look at the history of Aboriginal peoples and their relationship to this coastal environment, a setting that allowed for pursuits other than assuring survival. We're not hemmed in here. The ocean is open; we can breathe without barrier all the way to Japan. So a new question emerges: when writing under the influence of the natural surroundings, what blocks our creative processes? What stops the muse?

For me, it's fear: fear of laziness, fear of emptiness, fear of cliché. There is also the freezing fear of judgment, of being accused of sentimentalism (a core dread of mine), or that my work will be deemed anthropomorphic, oblivious to privilege, irrelevant to urban readers.

---

87   Greg Simison, in his introduction to "Kootenay Lake," in *Rocksalt*, ed. Mona Fertig and Harold Rhenisch.

Yet is there not some wisdom in embracing the inescapable? As author Fred Kaplan says, more than what can be counted and measured, there is what the meditative [artist] mind brings to bear in its attempt to find human significance in natural phenomena.[88]

I close my eyes, centre on my breath and look for significance around me. Judge me as you will. In the words of poet Maleea Acker, "I try to attend to small pieces of southern Vancouver Island ecosystems, in words or by action" while asking "what could possibly be an adequate response to the landscapes around me."[89] The challenge sustains me spiritually (and there's another baggage-encumbered word). I hope I receive this sustenance without being deaf to the voices that were here before me.

Up until very recently I feared that nature did my work for me, that I was no poet without it. After my entirely urban holiday in Europe, I did not write poems, just kept my journal as usual. Months later, back on my floathouse in the sound, I finished up a manuscript of nature poems, yet still felt chagrined to have created nothing out of all that legendary Italian art, the trip fading in my memory. So I went through my journal and drafted two "Europe" poems. Two entirely non-nature poems! No lichen, no rocks, no jellyfish! I swelled with pride and relief.

It is healthy to keep asking myself questions that push my practice as a writer. Whether it is with tunnel vision or a focussed response, I have to write what I know while facing my fears not just of unconsciousness and exclusivity but also of the imposing beauty of the far west.

I think back to Bowering's quote about terrible contradictions. The wild-yet-mild is not merely a fact about the place I live; it can mean exhilaration or depression, even life or death. I often feel deeply polarized within myself. Sometimes this can seem healthy and balanced and

---

88   Fred Kaplan, *Lincoln*, quoted in *Sky* magazine, February 2009, 88.
89   Maleea Acker, in her introdruction to "Tree Frogs," in *Rocksalt*, ed. Mona Fertig and Harold Rhenisch.

unpredictable. Other times it feels stressful. Nature has no need of me, but I have need of it. Summers I'm in a floathouse, off the grid, away from civilization, gasping from my forays into the tourist hub. Winters I'm in Tofino, gleefully connected to as many wires as a townie can be connected to. Half the year I am sedentary; the other, fixatedly fit. I even took up roller derby for a while. Lacing up my skates made up for all the hours of writing, sitting on my butt. I've been stamped both "nature girl" and punk rocker, and for a while I was also Red Tide— until a sprained ankle curbed that ambition. Like other writers, I'm industrious and rebellious, distracted and productive, damaged and healing, all with my bruised butterfly heart. I am not sure what this seasick, pendulous way of life does for my art. So far, writing happens without structure, without routine—but obsessively. Place imposes itself at random; creative response is obligatory. My plan is to follow the art, try to keep up with it, in whatever season.

Let's Mingle

⟶

Place is important but how could it not be? It matters the most
when you want to be here ... Enter the bramble of life. Observe a
thicket. Enjoy a poem.

—Al Rempel, in his introduction to
"Connective Tissue," in *Rocksalt*

I've challenged myself as an author to write poetry that doesn't
romanticize the natural world, which is something many Canadi-
an writers do very well. Consumer culture, large urban cities and
the way politics shape our lives interest me more than meandering
through a bramble patch.

—Sean Horlor, in his introduction to
"Fixer-Uppers," in *Rocksalt*

We always learn something in a thicket.

—Laurie Ricou,
Salal: Listening for the Northwest Understory

In the fiftieth issue of *subTerrain*, Peter Babiak said he was heartily sick
of the claim that "Vancouver's natural geography is vital to its literary

lifeblood."[90] He was reacting to a draft proposal to have that city designated a UNESCO City of Literature. Take its literary scene, he wrote, "toss in vague ideological mystifications about its super-natural natural environment, and you are left with intelligent 'bling' for the global creative class." Babiak was sitting in a cafeteria on Grouse Mountain with his niece when he wrote the article, having just hiked the Grind. Tourists at a nearby table were admiring the view, calling it *mystical*. They had evidently gotten there by gondola.

If there is animosity between urban and non-urban creatives (a word that might be more inclusive than "artists") on Canada's west coast, it's worth inquiring into. This coast is the place we all love and hate. It includes the urban, suburban, rural and wild. We all create, wherever we are, except when we're blocked—and we often blame our location and/or environment for the blockage, when we're not praising it as our muse. How are we, divided, to thrive in a conformist society?

Surely we all agree that the coast is blessed with impressive viewscapes of mountains and sea. But let us not write "as if all that's needed for literature to happen is a mystical junction of water, a rapid shift in elevation and trees."[91]

The last time I took a real hike, my knee needed surgery afterward. I live in the middle of nature and have no need to overly exert myself to experience it. Would I love it as much if I were stuck in it? Doubtful. I'd focus on returning to civilization, enjoy a hot bath and open my laptop to write a poem about what I saw. Does this invalidate my love for the wild? In the same issue of the magazine Daniel Francis implicates the more strenuous outdoor enthusiasts for the preposterous tourist slogan "British Columbia: The Best Place on Earth":

---

90   Peter Babiak, "Wordsworth on Grouse Mountain," *subTerrain* 50 (2008).
91   Ibid.

Many British Columbians are nature worshippers, happiest when they are kayaking down a white-water rapid or bounding along a mountain trail. They may approve of the slogan because they believe it. The rest of us are expected to swallow our embarrassment and go along with the illusion.[92]

Poet Don McKay notes that Canadians have "vexed and complicated relations to wilderness."[93] Clearly we take it out on each other. Is that what makes this place so meaningful for creatives? Conflict? If this conflict stems, as Patricia O'Connell Killen writes, from space and grandeur requiring "a rethinking of the meaning of the human person,"[94] perhaps by divvying up into sides that throw criticisms at each other—if, in fact, our bickering sustains art, do let's try *not* to get along.

⫧⌒⫧

At my suburban high school I went from nerd to hippie to punk. When I moved to Vancouver Island and joined the logging blockades I was called *hippie* again. It was a common insult; bumper stickers used to read "Think fast, hippie!" or "Hippies suck" or simply show a red line through the word *Hippies*. Even now if I slip up and call my still-urban friends hippies, they are deeply annoyed.

Yet they are the hip ones. I couldn't live with the pressure to be über-cool when I was young; it was a relief to leave the city, where I was surrounded by alternative, adventurous, artistic people. Warren attended an art college where, according to him, everyone wore black. "So pretentious," he says. "So I wore grey. Art school made me an activist."

92   Daniel Francis, "British Columbia: The Best Place on Earth," *subTerrain* 52, 2008.

93   Don McKay, introduction to *Open Wide a Wilderness: Canadian Nature Poems*, ed. Nancy Holmes (Waterloo, ON: Wilfrid Laurier University Press, 2009).

94   Patricia O'Connell Klein, "Memory, Novelty and Possibility in This Place, " in *Cascadia: The Elusive Utopia; Exploring the Spirit of the Pacific Northwest*, ed. Douglas Todd (Vancouver, BC: Ronsdale Press, 2008).

Personally, I needed more natural surroundings. I didn't know it then, but I needed them to heal. It was worth it for me to put myself outside the mainstream loop, or to admit there are always thousands of loops, and that it's too much stress to try and keep up.

After all, it is not all art and alternative culture out here. As artists, we put ourselves *out there*. We are outted by sharing our creations. And at the end of the road, we're out even farther. Tofino is the Pacific Rim Highway terminus. When urbanites write, we do not lambaste them for ignoring our realities. How can we, way out here, be a threat just by writing about the inconvenience and discomfort of being away from pavement? In his critique of several western books, Steven Poole wrote:

> In the case of the urban consumer of nature writing, of course, the mud is to be hosed off one's mental Range Rover immediately [once] one lifts one's eyes from the page and gives silent thanks for the civilised appurtenances of hot yoga and flat whites.[95]

It seems a given that the west coast inspires artistic expression and unique behaviours, not to mention an eclectic mix of spiritual beliefs, but it goes beyond that to ingredients of the left coast stereotype—one of relaxed, open views, privilege and laziness. But I want to look complacency in the eye and ask, can a culture of the fortunate also express itself as a culture of resistance? And I'm aware that whenever I say "we" of the coast, I am (unintentionally) likely excluding multiple cultures. Speaking only for myself, then, *what* is my culture as a creative person here in the far west of Canada? A possible answer: with good fortune comes my responsibility to declare resistance to conformity

---

95   Steven Poole, "Is our love of nature writing bourgeois escapism?" the *Guardian*, July 6, 2013.

and injustice. "Art contributes to a culture of resistance, which is what we're trying to build,"[96] said Gord Hill of the Art and Anarchy exhibit, a show in Vancouver that featured sculptures, carvings, drawings, jewellery and photography that challenged the 2010 Olympic games. Art and Anarchy dared its viewers to be more aware of their surroundings, such as the changes to Vancouver's Downtown Eastside as the Olympics preparations accelerated. There, community art was raised as walls between neighbourhoods and to disguise certain areas, make them more palatable. This exploitation of art and artists to both idealize and hide reality needed the alternatives of resistance and activism.

No doubt coastal creatives will continue to challenge each other, respectfully, I hope. It might be one way to thrive. The idea is not to enforce divisions but to keep ourselves awake, imaginative, productive. I am a page poet but I won't despise you for being a performance/spoken-word urban poet. I might admire you for belonging comfortably to the urban scene and making a name for yourself there; I won't purposely exclude you from a project I'm editing. In this province we are not so far apart. Nicholas Bradley wrote that "broadly successful environmentalism will have to find a way not to alienate CEOs, apartment-dwellers, and buyers of consumer goods. The city and the country are not always distant worlds."[97] We should mingle. Spoken-word poets don't have regular access to those in the publishing world, points out slam competitor RC Weslowski in *CV2*,[98] correcting my assumption that urban creatives have better opportunity.

We can read books printed by publishers who accept both urban and non-urban writers. We can look for writing and art that responds

---

96   Gord Hill, in Sarah Berman's article "Art and Anarchy: Artists give the Cultural Olympiad the middle finger," *The Dominion: news from the grassroots*, April 9, 2009, www.dominionpaper.ca/articles/2554 (accessed July 29, 2014).

97   Nicholas Bradley, review of *Writing the West Coast*, *Malahat Review*, Winter 2008.

98   RC Weslowski, interviewed by Steve Locke, *CV2* 36, no. 3, Winter 2014.

to nature in new ways and observe closely our own responses to this place. "The practice of being arrested by natural complexity and try-ing to act in response to that experience, that's the most important thing,"[99] writes Tim Lilburn.

⤚

Random Acts of Art in Tofino and Ucluelet, or RAATU, gives people an excuse to be uncommonly creative for one week out of the year, even if it only means dressing more outlandishly than usual. It provides an excuse to act out, get in touch with our inner exhibitionist, expose art to more people and people to more art.

It happens in April. People wear masks and walk in slow motion, or caper like clowns; one year someone stood absolutely still for an hour at an intersection under an umbrella on a sunny day, and Santa Claus went by on a bicycle. My random act was to dress punky and rollerskate inside the co-op grocery store, nearly getting myself kicked out. I wanted to shake things up a bit, wake the place up, have fun, make punk shui. By telephone from Vancouver, my sister pointed out that I could have knocked over an old lady.

I'm still teaching myself not to blush for somehow managing to live in one of the world's most privileged places, albeit close to First Nation artists who, on or off reserve, survive at Canada's lowest stan-dard of living. One artist, responding to a call for submissions from locations west of BC's mainland, simply said: "I can't afford to live west of the mainland." Island dwellers are privileged, yes, but ours is a privileged poverty. One artist told me that his yearly income is about $9,500. He lives here by luck, squatting, pet-sitting and frequently moving. Somehow in the chaos he practises art. He must, he says, be-cause it bursts out of him and he would die if he got in its way. Sounds

---

99   A Point of VIU, "Vancouver Island University Welcomes Celebrated Environmental Writer," www2.viu.ca/news/page.asp?ID=1586 (accessed July 24, 2014).

familiar. As do Kim Goldberg's eloquent, urban words in "Weather-grams," clearly expressing her need to live in the city: "I wanted to feel the sound of my words echoing in the cathedral of the underpass, bouncing off its pigeonstruck vault."[100]

BC may not be the best place on Earth. That's arguable. It's a big place, and art is a big practice. Gail Wells points out that the west coast's geography can be "as divisive as it is unifying, depending on the eye of the beholder."[101]

People who choose the city should not automatically ignore non-urban expression. People who have decided to leave the city should not look down their noses at what they couldn't handle. Judgments, after all. Differences are ours to celebrate.

100 Kim Goldberg, "Weathergrams," in *Living Artfully: Reflections from the Far West Coast*, ed. Anita Sinner and Christine Lowther (Toronto: The Key Publishing House Inc., 2012). ISBN 9781926780146.

101 Gail Wells, "Nature-based Spirituality in Cascadia: Prospects, Pitfalls, and Observations," in *Cascadia: The Elusive Utopia; Exploring the Spirit of the Pacific Northwest*, ed. Douglas Todd (Vancouver, BC: Ronsdale Press, 2008).

POSTSCRIPTS

I leave the VHF radio on every night, emergency channel 16. In case of tsunami warning. My plan is to get to shore as quickly as possible, hit the trail and hike as far as the bog. There I must leave the trail, cut across the bog and head for the nearest peak of the Camel. I'll have to bushwhack, with my carefully assembled kit of water, cellphone, radio, food, clothing, blankets, matches, supreme flashlight, etc.

Except that I have no emergency kit, and how could I dream of following that rough trail at night, even with a torch?

Trail? What trail? Last time I looked for it—tried to follow it—I ended flailing in thorns, clinging panting to salal, filling a sandal with my own piss, my other foot up to the ankle in moss. *This forest is indifferent to me*, I realized, *or worse. It no longer wants to be seen, if it ever did.* The bogs with their flowers and bear prints, the frogs in their pools, the sweet gale field, the beginning of the lake: not to be seen, heard, smelled, felt again. It's gone. It doesn't love me. There is no trail. The wild has reclaimed it.

There is an ugly controversy regarding whether humans belong in wilderness, or merely mess it up. Some believe no place is truly wild unless humans don't go there. I know that wild animals prefer a habitat with fewer people. The rewilding of the trail may be good for this place. It may even be good for me, if cougars are about. Yet I mourn.

Of course I could borrow a machete, become a trailblazer, with permission. (Better a trail than a road!) But on September 24, 2013, a lone wolf made an appearance onshore. I first heard her howling on the far side of the bay, then a while later near the oyster farm, then on this side. Finally, I saw her from my kitchen window. She had to have swum from the bay's western point to the oyster farm's islet, finally landing on the eastern point, all in record time. An incredible fitness level. Close to the rushing creek, she turned sharply when I carefully opened my sliding glass door a millimetre. Extraordinary sense of hearing. I read somewhere of a belief that wolves can hear the clouds gliding by overhead.

The shore, forest, bog, lake, hill are her home. She has no other. And she is special. The Vancouver Island wolf is endemic to the island; its elimination from this island, and the smaller surrounding islands like Meares, would mean permanent extinction from the wild. So, in what state is the wolves' home? Climate change, it seems, is already altering the forest we fought for. It's a familiar refrain, but I have observed it with my own senses. The moss is receding, there's less rain and fewer salmon spawning. Proposed mines threaten the surrounding undeveloped mountains, their rare beauty and integrity. Fish farms are polluting the ocean I love. As controversial oil-transporting schemes fill the news, many residents remember 1989, the year oil coated local shores. That was before my time—not my tale to tell, and I hope it never will be.

Every once in a while the Clayoquot Sound Conservation Alliance (CSCA) meets here to review the current status of intact areas, share information and protection strategies. The CSCA is a group of activists from Greenpeace, Forest Ethics and other large environmental organizations—plus our own little Friends of Clayoquot Sound with its single employee. In between, there are many multi-group conference calls. No one is forgetting how precious and important this place is, even while other locales also deserve defence. An action history:

1984: MEARES ISLAND
—First significant logging blockade in BC history

1988: SULPHUR PASS
—35 arrests

1992: CLAYOQUOT ARM
—65 arrests

1993: KENNEDY RIVER
—932 arrests

1996: RANKIN COVE
—Joint FOCS and Greenpeace action

2003: LOSTSHOE FLATS
—Heli-logging blockade

201X: TRANQUIL CREEK?[102]

I live tied and anchored to Meares Island. In 1984, Clayoquot's first blockade occurred on its other side, at C'is-a-qis, when Tla-o-qui-ahts and non-Natives united to stand against MacMillan Bloedel. In 2014 we marked thirty years since this event, and since the Tla-o-qui-ahts' declaration of Meares, or *Wah-nah-jus–Hilth-hoo-is*, as a Tribal Park. On Easter Sunday a feast in the Tofino Community Hall celebrated this anniversary. After welcoming prayers, drumming and a masked dancer, there were speeches and shared memories.

---

102   Source: Friends of Clayoquot Sound.

Leigh Hilbert addressed the crowd, telling us how he and Joe Martin had both been working for MacBlo when they heard about the company's plans to clearcut Meares. Joe was a logger, Leigh a road engineer; the Meares plan would mean more work for them. However, having already seen some of the devastation caused by clearcutting and now feeling shocked at the danger hanging over the beloved island, both quit their positions and informed their communities of the company's intentions.

MacBlo itself stated those intentions at a meeting held in Tofino's elementary school to First Nations, provincial and municipal government representatives, environmental groups and local residents. Linda Baril stood up at that meeting, shaking. She had never spoken in public before. Two of her children were on either side of her. The company rep was saying not to worry, that logging equipment wasn't on its way to the island yet. "Your machines," said Linda, "will have to run over me and my children." Today she remembers something palpably changing in the room then. As precious as Meares was, this was about more than one island. This was a chance to defend the future for everyone's kids and grandkids.

Also legendary is the story of how Chief Moses Martin addressed the loggers from shore as they attempted to dock their boat on the island. The mist was curling around the forest, seeping in and out of the trees. Moses stood firm and swept out his arm to encompass the scene. "This is our garden," he said. "There will be no logging here today." Then he crossed his arms, a picture of unquestionable authority. The loggers were welcome, but their chainsaws were not.

As I sat listening on Easter 2014 to the official Declaration of Tribal Parks—there are now four in the sound—read aloud in full, I was impressed by its strong environmental stance. Of course, Tla-o-qui-aht traditional ways honour peoples and the environment as one, so what was read was merely sanity. Phrases like "healthy homelands," "healthy people," "co-existence," even terms like "carbon credits" are all part of declaring a Tribal Park. I watched dances with eagle feathers and rattles, a parent and child dancing in cedar bark ribbon costumes and women in fringed black capes dancing to a loud drum and men's proud voices. I watched children and babies enjoying the music and spectacle. In a free report I picked up on my way out titled *Welcome to Tla-o-qui-aht Tribal Parks!* I read:

> Even after many generations of Tla-o-qui-aht people had lived within our Ha'wiih (Chiefs) territories, we still enjoyed a fully intact rainforest until European contact ... Instead of following the heavy industrial model of unsustainable resource extraction, we aim to benefit from our territories by enjoying and respecting them, rather than exploiting them. This is where you come in![103]

The report goes on to describe park highlights as tourist attractions and a means of practising low-impact use of traditional lands and the sea. After all their people have lost, pride and sharing are expressed, not anger and pain. It was truly humbling to sit in the crowded hall and be told over and over again how grateful they were to us relative newcomers of European descent for our support.

ᴛᴡ

I'm not sure if any of the ceremonial masks I saw that day were wolf masks. I couldn't tell. One of the reasons First Nations peoples pay attention to animals is because animals know some things before humans do. If birds and other critters are behaving strangely, an earth-

---

103 "The History of Tla-o-qui-aht Tribal Parks," *Welcome to Tla-o-qui-aht Tribal Parks!* 32, no. 6 (Tla-o-qui-aht Tribal Parks and the Wilderness Committee, Summer 2013), http://wildernesscommittee.org/all/files/publications/2013_tla-o-qui-aht_Paper-Web-2.pdf (accessed July 24, 2014).

quake may be imminent. If they flee to higher ground, a tsunami. My float is at the end of an inlet, which would act as a funnel for the wave. Riding the roof is inadvisable because it's not high enough, and my house could quickly be turned to matchsticks by churning surges full of debris. It seems the only feasible idea is to flee to shore and climb a high tree, though trees can be knocked over. Worst-case scenario: it could happen at high tide, snapping the lines, or at night, during a storm. I must find and purchase some of that glow-in-the-dark flagging tape I learned about at the last tsunami information presentation.

No, absolute worst-case scenario is if the quake comes when I am halfway down the inlet in my little boat. I have no plan for that.

I wonder if I could ever hate the ocean. If it destroyed my home, killed loved ones, traumatized me, wrecked the town, pulled trees down? Could I forgive it? Would I ever be hurt so deeply I'd never want to look at it again?

A tsunami is caused by an earthquake. What am I going to do, hate the Earth? Nature has a bloody side. I've always known that and, except for one or two poems, I've chosen to focus on the "nicer" ways of Mother Earth. Not when hoping to protect her, though. I want to defend and protect the whole chaotic beast, including the unpopular, the forgotten and the scruffy green growth surrounded by pavement.

Down through time, hundreds of Canadians and others have congregated to volunteer their protection of places. Earth has benefited from both locals and visitors actually laying down their freedom to defend it from the destruction of greed. The relatively intact forests of Clayoquot Sound are in debt to these people, wherever they dwell now.

Complacency is the enemy of both forest and ocean. Good news is not something to rest on, but to build on. When I first moved here humpback whales were a species of the past, extirpated by hunting. Incredibly—at first I didn't believe the reports—they have come back. Sea otters were extirpated by the fur trade. They have also been returning, slowly, after being reintroduced up north. Basking sharks were ruthlessly slaughtered by the Fisheries Department; in the autumn of 2013, one was sighted and photographed. Such comebacks always feel like extinct animals returning to life—a second chance.

⊰

At the end of another tourist season the Ucluelet Aquarium releases an octopus off the dock at Tofino's Meares Landing, where it was caught half a year ago. It has grown large. When the lid of the bin is removed the animal hesitates; then its powerful arms uncurl and it slides sideways and lunges for freedom. Alien grace takes the cephalopod quickly out of sight: it sinks down under the dock, away from captivity, into deep water, back where it belongs.

Only by entering the ocean and feeling that complete immersion do I become part of this bay, forest and mountain where my home is anchored. For years I was curious about my obsession simply because not everyone shares it. Many are happy to soak in the hot water without ever putting so much as a toe into the cold. Then Chief Earl Maquinna George, in *Living On the Edge: Nuu-Chah-Nulth History From an Ahousaht Chief's Perspective*, described how for his people (whose territory is just north of here), immersing was "cleansing of the soul, cleansing of the body, cleansing of the mind, cleansing of evil spirits … exchanged for the strong will to live and fight."[104] The water, so cold, changes everything. Day or night, each time I emerge from the ocean I feel reborn.

---

104 Chief Earl Maquinna George, *Living On the Edge: Nuu-Chah-Nulth History From an Ahousaht Chief's Perspective* (Winlaw, BC: Sono Nis Press, 2005).

PHOTO WARREN RUDD.

Acknowledgements

Some of these essays, or earlier versions of them, previously appeared in *Writing the West Coast* (Ronsdale Press, 2008); *Living Artfully: Reflections from the Far West Coast* (The Key Publishing House, 2012); *Monday* magazine (Victoria); *Animal Studies Journal* (University of Wollongong, Australia); *Wild Moments: Adventures with Animals of the North* (University of Alaska Press, 2009); *Tofino Time*; the now-defunct *Gulf Island Gazette* (the *Gig*); the *Beaver*; and the *Vancouver Sun*. Deep thanks to all of the publishers and editors involved. As always, I owe a debt to the members of the Clayoquot Writers Group and its alumni, particularly my greatest fan, poet Sherry Marr. A surprising quantity of what I learned about my own family was researched by someone outside it: the brilliant Christine Wiesenthal, author of *The Half-Lives of Pat Lowther* and editor of *The Collected Works of Pat Lowther*. Kudos to the extremely helpful person who found the 1986 Capilano College course outline for Sociology 210, whose name, unfortunately, was somehow lost. I also feel grateful for the day jobs that both prevent and allow my writing; thank you, employers Reflecting Spirit Gallery (Signy Cohen, art goddess) and Tofino General Hospital. So many friends and acquaintances have helped me in so many ways, both little and large, that I could fill a book with names.

It's hard to do justice to Jane Silcott, my editor, whose mad skills, patience and tact were acts of love and magic. My publisher, Vici Johnstone, was and is nothing less than a god, and her publicist, Andrea

Routley, is equally worthy of worship. Holly Vestad and Kathleen Fraser deserve their own altars also. I was so blessed to have such a team; sometimes I still have to pinch myself. Regarding my good fortune of having had books published, I doubt I would ever have come this far in such reasonable time without the timely intervention of my friend Anita Sinner. But this book is for my sisters, Beth and Kathy.

CHRISTINE LOWTHER has been a lifelong activist and a resident of Clayoquot Sound since 1992. She is the co-editor of two collections of essays, *Living Artfully: Reflections from the Far West Coast* (The Key Publishing House, 2012) and *Writing the West Coast: In Love with Place* (Ronsdale Press, 2008), and the author of three books of poetry, *My Nature* (Leaf Press, 2010), *Half-Blood Poems* (Zossima Press, 2011) and *New Power* (Broken Jaw Press, 1999). Most recently, several of her poems appear in *Force Field: 77 Women Poets of British Columbia* (Mother Tongue, 2013).